WORD OF THE WEEK

A framework for unlocking your willPower

Dear Kristina,
I hope this book allows you to feel the shift in your willPower.
Best, Sarah

Sarah Ingmanson

Copyright © 2015 Sarah Ingmanson.

All rights reserved. No part of this book may be used or reproduced by any means, graphic, electronic, or mechanical, including photocopying, recording, taping or by any information storage retrieval system without the written permission of the author except in the case of brief quotations embodied in critical articles and reviews.

Balboa Press books may be ordered through booksellers or by contacting:

Balboa Press
A Division of Hay House
1663 Liberty Drive
Bloomington, IN 47403
www.balboapress.com
1 (877) 407-4847

Because of the dynamic nature of the Internet, any web addresses or links contained in this book may have changed since publication and may no longer be valid. The views expressed in this work are solely those of the author and do not necessarily reflect the views of the publisher, and the publisher hereby disclaims any responsibility for them.

The author of this book does not dispense medical advice or prescribe the use of any technique as a form of treatment for physical, emotional, or medical problems without the advice of a physician, either directly or indirectly. The intent of the author is only to offer information of a general nature to help you in your quest for emotional and spiritual well-being. In the event you use any of the information in this book for yourself, which is your constitutional right, the author and the publisher assume no responsibility for your actions.

Any people depicted in stock imagery provided by Thinkstock are models, and such images are being used for illustrative purposes only.
Certain stock imagery © Thinkstock.

Print information available on the last page.

ISBN: 978-1-5043-4557-6 (sc)
ISBN: 978-1-5043-4559-0 (hc)
ISBN: 978-1-5043-4558-3 (e)

Library of Congress Control Number: 2015919101

Balboa Press rev. date: 12/07/2015

Contents

PREFACE	vii
FOCUS	1
TRUTH	7
RENEW	13
DETERMINATION	19
PURPOSE	24
ACCEPT	29
EMOTION	34
HOPE	40
SEARCH	47
INSPIRE	53
LISTEN	61
TRUST	66
CLARITY	72
IF	78
CONFIDENCE	83
RISK	88
CHALLENGE	95
CONTROL	102
BALANCE	109
STRENGTH	117
THRIVE	125
ACHIEVE	131
ENGAGE	138
PASSION	144
SURPRISE	149
REACH	154

FREEDOM	161
RESPECT	166
BELIEVE	171
COMMITMENT	177
POWER	183
VISION	188
DIGNITY	194
VIRTUE	200
INTEGRITY	206
FAITH	212
REMEMBER	217
DEPTH	224
CHANGE	230
PEACE	237
PATIENCE	243
PATIENCE	248
PRECISION	253
TRANSFORM	258
EXPLORE	263
SURRENDER	268
VALUE	275
GRATITUDE	281
WILLPOWER	287
GRACE	293
PREPARE	298
SAVOR	302

Preface

The Word of the Week is a framework for empowerment... your empowerment. When we limit fitness to what we do in the gym or the kitchen exclusively, we fall short... at a soul level. To say that the mind-body connection is relevant is a gross understatement. When we lose the strength of our mind-body connection, we lose ourselves... literally. I can attest.

In 2006, my frequent flier miles seemed to be accumulating at a rate similar to my ER visits. From Las Vegas to Tokyo to NY, could I survive a business trip without frequenting the ER? The answer seemed to be "no" even though, by all outward appearances, I was a fit, healthy, happy, and successful woman in her early thirties.

Outward appearances can be deceiving, though. When your soul knows differently, your body eventually decides it will no longer put up with the abuse this disconnect is creating.

When we are misaligned with our purpose, a part of ourselves dies. Enter willPower here. (Yes, that's willPower with a capital "P".)

Up until then, I had shunned fitness classes as a fitness format for the lazy and undisciplined female. Certainly, not me. As a former competitive figure skater, I can pretty much count on two hands the number of days I took off from the ice between the age of nine and 22. In college, my alarm went off at 4:30am every morning so I could make 5:30am practice. Discipline was my strong suit. Socialization with people at the gym... was not.

However, even on the treadmill, I was still "working". Whether I was drafting an email to Tokyo in my head or religiously monitoring my BlackBerry (because it *was* 2007!) throughout the run, I wasn't following my doctor's orders. Actually, his first suggestion was to quit my job, but he could tell by my body language and response ("No way, I love my job!") that he wouldn't win that argument. So, he challenged me to make my job more sustainable... and then, suggested the gym.

A few months later, I was using up my last weekend at the gym because my neuroticism had decided that the 15 minute drive to the gym was too far from my desk and a treadmill at home would do the trick. On this particular Saturday, my anxiety had been particularly bothersome and I arrived a little later than usual. As I was putting my belongings away in the locker room, your prototypical fitness instructor (read: perfectly put together, obnoxiously happy, glowing blonde) approached me to say that I had to try this new class. I shook my head and explained that I don't do classes, but she wasn't taking no for an answer.

My first BodyPump class gave me that aha moment of what I was missing: a fitness outlet that would provide complete diversion from work. My weekly BodyPump habit quickly ramped up to 3-4 classes a week whenever I was home. I loved boarding the long flight to Narita with soreness in my muscles. I also found that the jet lag went away a little faster "on BodyPump" when I returned.

By that summer, the group fitness director had noticed me in class and invited me to become an instructor. As I began explaining my job and travel schedule, I surprised myself when a "yes" fell out of my mouth. Thus, began my love affair with fitness... classes.

Adding "fitness instructor" to my resume made absolutely no sense... I mean, no logical sense, but, in my personal (and observed) experience, the "good" stuff never does. Practically speaking, I was in Tokyo half of every month. In other words, I could never have a class on the schedule... and, besides, why would I bother? The pay was a measly $20/hr, which paled in comparison to my $200k Wall Street salary. Also, my days, nights, and weekends were consumed by work, so it wasn't that I needed to add anything to an already overflowing plate. But, the voice inside said, "yes", so I listened.

The voice inside is usually loudest when it is saving your life and steering you back to your purpose. Note to self: always listen.

From there, the certifications began to accumulate... BodyPump, BodyCombat, spin, dance... I even signed up for a certification without having experienced the class before: willPower & grace®. A fellow instructor encouraged me toward it. "The founder, Stacey Lei Krauss is the sh--... she's just amazing," he assured me. So, I did. He was right. Thus, this book.

So, let me tell you about this book. It originates from The willPower Method® and the "Word of the Week" (WoW). As a willPower instructor, I am expected to introduce the WoW into my class as a centering theme and a creative focus for my cues. To spread the "word", I would post a quote with a little blurb about the WoW at the beginning of every week.

What started off as a weekly Facebook post turned into a weekly blog on willpowerlife.com. Now, I am taking it one step further and transforming it into a framework.

A framework for unlocking your willPower.

Within the WoW, this book encourages you to think about the parts of yourself... your energy centers... your archetypes. There happen to be seven, which corresponds nicely with the number of days in the week. By applying this framework to the WoW, you will bring more deliberate focus to your willPower... and to perhaps the disconnect that is keeping you from true mind-body connection and soul alignment with your life purpose.

Your energy centers are clustered along your spinal column. These energy centers form chakras. I deliberately chose archetypes to represent these chakras because a visible cue can communicate in a way that words simply cannot.

The Warrior represents your Root Chakra, honored with survival, self-preservation, your physical identity, the mother inside you. This is where you ground yourself in your body and heal ancestral issues.

The Lover represents your Sacral Chakra, focused on pleasure, your emotional identity. This is where you overcome feelings of shame and guilt.

Word of the Week

The Athlete represents your Solar Plexus Chakra, grounded in your willpower, your strength, positioned right above your navel… therefore your core identity. This is where you develop your personal power and self-worth, balance the ego, and learn to create healthy boundaries.

The Healer represents your Heart Chakra, encompassed in love, your social identity. This is where you feel compassion and heal yourself and others through your loving presence.

The Artist represents your Throat Chakra, involved in how you communicate to the world, your creative identity, your self-expression. This is where you learn to speak your truth.

The Sage represents your Brow Chakra, housing your intuition, your imagination, your intellectual identity. This is where you learn to honor your vision and see past, present, and future in a wise way.

Word of the Week

The Angel represents your Crown Chakra, nurturing your spirituality, your spiritual identity, and your connectedness to all there is. This is where you see the bigger lesson or message in your life and feel the connection you have to all that is.

The words are sequenced in a deliberate order, but that does not mean you have to follow this sequence. Maybe as you glance through the table of contents, a word jumps out at you as "your" WoW for this week. Similarly, for the archetypes. I list them from the bottom up, but you might want to work from the top down or jump around depending on what you have lined up for that day. For example, on a day where you plan to have a big workout or a big meeting, the Athlete or Warrior might be good choices. The day after said workout or meeting, Lover or Sage might resonate the most.

Just as we say in willPower & grace ("Make the workout work for you"), make this book work for you.

With love, willPower, and gratitude,

Sarah

FOCUS

a.k.a. conspiracy theory at its finest

When focus meets desire, it becomes a done deal. Don't believe me? Try. I mean, don't *try*, *do*. Action and belief are essential ingredients of focus.

Focus brings your desires to you in the fastest and best possible ways. Doors start opening and people... events... circumstances all seem to lend a helping hand to your personal cause. Conspiracy theory at its finest.

When you live moment to moment, you are in a constant state of reactivity to whatever life is throwing at you. When you have goals... or I prefer to call them *desires with focus*, there is a plan in place. From this strong stance, your greatness is activated.

We need to develop our focus to see two things at once. What is on our proverbial plate today and that dream, goal, desire that drives us uniquely. Our focus helps us decide what is best to do with the current dish of today, and cloaks us in our willPower to navigate around the daily temptations to react... to succumb... and to settle for less. Shortchanging our longer term goals for immediate gratification is a dispirited disservice to ourselves. So, wrap yourself up in your willPower as you head for the door... and focus.

"The key to success is to focus our conscious mind on things we desire not things we fear." ~Brian Tracy

FOCUS on your breath.

Let your focus symbolize your desire to live… the connection to your presence. Notice your breath at various points throughout the day. Find the power in your breath to soothe you and to keep your focus firmly rooted.

FOCUS on the feeling.

Let your internal compass help guide your micro-decisions throughout the day. Start that book when your mind craves it. Turn to that big project at the optimal time of your day… despite whatever is coming through your inbox. In your workouts, ask yourself where should I be feeling this? Heighten the mind-muscle connection in all you do. By the way, willPower is a type of muscle…

FOCUS on beauty... around you... in you, and of you.

Go beyond merely noticing beauty. Take as much time as you need to soak it in and to feel it within yourself. Then, move and communicate from that place of beauty.

FOCUS on gratitude.

Gratitude is a game-changer. As you move from a scarcity mindset ("I don't have enough...") to an abundance mindset ("I am so blessed for..."), watch how things shift and flourish. This is particularly important if you're putting ourselves through the paces (athletic or not) in some area of your life. For example, putting in extra hours at work, driving to chemotherapy, going the distance in your marathon training, sticking to your fitness lifestyle even when the couch... or a food temptation... beckons.

FOCUS on the newsfeed that matters.

How would your decisions change if you weren't trying to please anyone but yourself? If the only "approval" or "like" that truly mattered came from within? If you commonly feel compelled to please others, this is an important step for you.

FOCUS on love… self-love… love emanating from and toward you.

The absence of love is fear… and that's all it is. So, when you feel less than loving, ask yourself, "What am I afraid of?" It may not be immediately obvious, but let the answers surface. Then, see if you can let go of that fear and trust yourself… to love again.

FOCUS on whatever it is you are doing.

Perfect the art of single-tasking. Our brains simply cannot single-task, so we should not attempt to either! Easier said than done, I realize. The artist in us has a beautiful, but wandering mind. One idea leads to a next. And, in this era where the weapons of mass distraction are truly everywhere with increasingly shinier bells and whistles, it truly becomes willPower-ful to stay grounded. You are in charge, though… or you can be. Turn off the disrupters and control your notifications. How "available" you are is an important ingredient in your creativity and a signal to the Universe at how serious you are about said endeavor... career... life.

FOCUS on the present moment as a puzzle piece to the finish.

Even though we have a goal or vision that we are working toward, we understand that the future is manifested by our micro-steps and micro-decisions today.

FOCUS on stillness... the gap... the pause.

Carve out some silence in your day first thing in the morning... even if you have to set your alarm for 15 minutes earlier. When we strengthen our intuition, we sharpen our focus, which allows us to bring our desires into play faster.

FOCUS on positive expansion.

What we focus on expands—in both good and bad ways. Notice where your mind is drifting throughout the day and the expectations you have going into things. Do you expect the airport to be a nightmare? And then, is it? Yes, exactly. I love airports. Just saying...

TRUTH

Reuniting with Truth

"Truth be told..." Yes, please. "To be honest..." Oh, thank goodness. I've always wondered the point of these introductory phrases. I mean, why do we split up with truth in the first place?

Truth is vulnerability on a platter. Truth is refreshing, occasionally painful, but most of all, it is liberating to both the giver and receiver... to say it like it is... like it really is.

Truth is self-recognition. It's being consistent internally and externally, and giving yourself the permission to speak, breathe, and... live your truth. Truth-telling is when you expose your divinity along with your humanity. When you let the mask slip along with the constant self-censoring of "Am I saying the right thing?" "Do I look good?" "Do they love me?", realizing that your imperfections make you real and approachable.

Herein lies the truth. We love vulnerability in others, but we are scared to death of it in ourselves.

Truth is not needing to validate your feelings and desires. It's never making yourself "wrong" for wanting to do x or feeling y or being attracted to z. It's when you deny the truth to yourself or to the world that things begin to go haywire.

Truth-seeking mantras begin the process of cleansing our truth, which is ensconced in the throat chakra. Use these as a guide to opening up your truth within.

I could improve my health if I _____.

Yikes, but yes, the warrior is concerned with survival. And, true, one body, one life. Purify the vessel, improve not just the length but the quality of your life experience.

If money weren't an object, I would _____.

The Warrior is ever-concerned with survival. Sometimes… too often, it becomes plain ol' life-inhibiting. How can you bring the essence of what you want into your life today? Think vision board and expense review.

Word of the Week

I have time for _____.

Insert activity that you love, but tend to make yourself feel guilty or wrong for doing. In relationships, we are sometimes tempted to shut this part of ourselves down. Whether the person in your life doesn't share the same passion or you feel you are wrong for taking time for yourself… stop, drop, and listen. Sometimes, the best thing we can do for our loved ones is to seek our own happiness. They feel it and we feel better. Win-win.

I make self-care a priority in my life.

How do you? When do you? Can you add some more this week and every week going forward?

I am worthy of my desire to _____.

Permission to pursue your greatness here. Think big. Too many of us undershoot in the realm of what is possible.

I talk the talk and walk the walk of who I am and who I aspire to be.

Want to be promoted to VP at work? Step 1... start acting like one!

I listen to the truth in others.

Stop and listen... really listen. What are they trying to tell you? Listen closely and find what is being revealed one level deeper. Try communicating at the soul level... as in, heart-to-heart.

Word of the Week

Who I am doesn't change or depend upon with whom I am interacting.

Listen to your voice and how it reveals your truth. Does it change pitch, crack, or stutter around certain people or in certain situations? Do you stop yourself from adding to the conversation out of fear of sounding stupid or unworthy? Or, do you find yourself rambling on when you're nervous or uncomfortable with the silence? Heighten your awareness around your voice today. Be curious. See what it reveals to you… and to the world.

I find my eyes in the mirror first and foremost.

In the studio mirror, in the bathroom mirror… find your eyes and check in with yourself. See what others may not. See what is going on. You are the expert on you.

Sarah Ingmanson

This year, I will _____.

Get creative. Be audacious and bold. The Universe loves boldness and truth-telling.

RENEW

Before the expiration date... RENEW

Things go stale... unless we renew. That fresh loaf of French bread is disgusting the next day. Better eat that sushi tonight or you might end up with salmonella tomorrow.

With food, it's more obvious. Or, even when it's not, the regulators step in so there is an expiration date imprinted on the milk carton. For our safety. But, what about other things that "feed" us? Like our workouts, our diets... our relationships?

Are you drawn to new shiny things? My daughter is. She loves jewelry... gold chains in particular... but, your hair will do, too. At her age and stage, attraction to newness represents curiosity and learning. For the rest of us, it can be problematic. Problematic when it only scratches the surface or attempts to Band-Aid a wound that requires stitches.

In set position, we renew our stance for lifting... in just the same way I would line up the blade of my back foot perfectly perpendicular to the blade of my front foot before pushing off to a figure eight. You see, before any deliberate endeavor, you position yourself anew... to make new again... to renew. For how we start dictates how we finish. When we renew, we literally and figuratively reset the expiration date on ourselves. Insert willPower here. We must renew these things for ourselves before they expire... or we expire in the process.

Sarah Ingmanson

RENEW your body through different foods, flavors, and textures.

Eating the same thing over and over—no matter how healthy—leads to stagnation in the body and can also lead to temporary food allergies. Get out of the food rut. It can be as easy as throwing beets into the evening salad, baking acorn squash because it is in season, or adding some antioxidant-packed blueberries to breakfast oatmeal or pancakes. Did you know that avocado with coconut, lime, and vanilla protein powder resembles a key lime pie shake?

RENEW your power stance.

Ground yourself through your feet and energetically draw up through your inner thighs and core. Can you lift your toes? All 10 of them?

Plan your next vacation.

Word of the Week

Lack of vacation is the leading cause of "expiration" in a relationship. Enough said!

RENEW your workouts.

While repetition does lead to results, we need to introduce stimulus to grow. As a group fitness instructor, that is my job. As the consumer in your self- or trainer-directed workouts, make sure that is the case.

RENEW your confidence by attuning your body to it.

Just like in true set-position, draw your shoulders up, back, and around. Brace through your mid-section, and line your feet directly under your hips.

RENEW your commitment to a strong core in plank practice.

Core renewal gets to the essence of change and transformation. By heightening the awareness associated with engaging your abs... your core... the area where your solar plexus, the willPower chakra, is located.

RENEW your self-healing mechanisms by declaring an intention every day in the mirror or your journal.

Watch healing unfold as your action matches the intention.

RENEW the vow to yourself first and foremost.

Say what you mean and mean what you say.

Word of the Week

RENEW your vision by watching the sunrise.

Dedicate it to your renewal.

RENEW your view.

Take the long way home. Look with new eyes at your commute, the walk with your dog, a brisk winter jog or a cozy drive with the heat cranked up.

RENEW every day.... every breath offers us the opportunity to renew.

Sarah Ingmanson

A New Year symbolizes renewal, but we are the ones who ultimately decide when or how we renew ourselves. We don't need a New Year to find symbols of renewal when we observe the sun rise above the horizon or notice the inhale following the exhale.

DETERMINATION

Where the rubber meets the road... DETERMINATION

Desire fills us with creative fuel, but determination is where the rubber meets the road... even when the road is not visible.

Clutching the steering wheel more tightly as I notice a string of cars in pile-up after pile-up on the major interstate. Can these people not drive? I used to wonder with my East Coast sense of driving superiority. But soon thereafter, my car slid across the lane and my brakes failed to grip at the stoplight, and I realized I wasn't in Kansas anymore... or Boston for that matter. Rain in Vegas is as treacherous as ice in Boston.

For most of us, rain doesn't stop us from venturing out. We adjust. We buffer in more time and become extra vigilant. Not paralyzed and stuck, but alert and focused. There's a big difference. Determination gives us the strength to see past obstacles, rather than getting swallowed up in them. Determination sees poor road conditions as part of the journey and opportunities... opportunities to maneuver more expertly, to become more flexible, to gain valuable experience... to increase our willPower.

Determination is knowing why you are doing something. It is clear, decisive, inspired, honest action. With determination, we understand that the goal is not to stop change, it is to invite change... change within ourselves.

Therefore, this week's practice accelerates change and strengthens our willPower from head to toe… from inspired heart of self to inspiring heart of another.

DETERMINE what you are not going to do.

Put your stake in the ground. Say no to that project, class, activity, which no longer excites you.

DETERMINE your rest and downtime.

Literally, factor it in. Schedule it. Otherwise, you'll force it through sickness or injury.

Word of the Week

DETERMINE what you are going to give up.

Sometimes you can't have what is in front of you if you're not willing to let go of what's behind you.

DETERMINE your compensation for meeting your goals.

Yes, "pay" yourself as you would reward a star performer that works for you. Determine your compensation before setting out. The athlete knows his/her self-worth during contract talks…

DETERMINE how you want to feel and let those desired feeling(s) guide your decisions throughout the day.

If you want to feel loved, make loving decisions. If you want to feel accomplished, make decisions aligned with accomplishing.

DETERMINE your response to various scenarios.

Anticipate conflict and determine how you will respond without sacrificing your dignity or self-worth. We can't predict everything, but there is no reason to be blind-sided either.

DETERMINE your self-investment plan.

Just like a company needs to invest in property, plant, and equipment (PP&E) for future growth so do we. Sign up for that class, hire a coach, learn a new language, art, or craft. Trigger your creativity.

DETERMINE key milestones or minimum thresholds to reach goals in the important areas of your life.

Word of the Week

Think New Year resolutions, professional development, fitness goals, personal aspirations. What do you want to accomplish… really?

DETERMINE why your Sage's goals are so important to you.

Is self-love and personal passion fueling your determination… or is something else?

DETERMINE your destiny.

Free will is a beautiful thing. Don't forget to activate it with your determination.

PURPOSE

Seeing the target... PURPOSE

目的 (pronounced *mokuteki*) is Japanese for purpose. Two kanji characters: the first one symbolizes "eye"; the second symbolizes "target". Assembled next to each other and we *see the target*. Literally and figuratively, that is purpose.

In a fitness class, is it better to be the instructor or the participant? When you're the instructor, the great thing is you know what's coming up. The bad thing is... you know what's coming up! 100 more squats? 24 more push-ups? Tricep dips to failure? As the participant, you have no idea. Ignorance can be bliss. It can also be scary and downright frustrating. When you live purposefully, you become the instructor... of your life. You build awareness, accountability, and hopefully, acceptance for everything going on in your life... the good, the bad, the drama, the peace.

"I did that."

A single statement that can be both freeing and terrifying. When we realize how much we are involved with what happens to us, we start to choose differently.

"Thank you for showing me what I don't want."

Word of the Week

Powerful, life-changing stuff when we realize what we don't want. Contrast that sets us up to choose differently next time.

When babies don't want to eat what is presented to them on a spoon in front of their mouths, they scrunch up their noses, close their eyes, and shoot one arm across to karate chop said spoonful away (as I recall, sometimes away... more often, all over their mothers!) We could learn from that. When we continue to eat the disagreeable spoonfuls presented to us, we deceive ourselves into a life by default. We ignore our inner wisdom and poison our bodies with undesirable tastes.

So, this week, keep asking yourself about the purpose of said activity, said spoonful, said person in front of you. When you think in terms of purpose, your thought process becomes more focused, your decisions more succinct, your life more on point.

When we align our lives with purpose, we become who we were always meant to be.

The PURPOSE of this food on my plate is _____.

The PURPOSE of this injury, setback, scandal is _____.

The PURPOSE of this purchase, appointment, vacation, indulgence is _____.

The PURPOSE of the outfit I choose to wear today is _____.

The PURPOSE of this work, project, class, business trip, meeting, competition is _____.

The PURPOSE of this exercise, movement, activity is _____.

Word of the Week

The PURPOSE of this relationship, friendship, opponent is _____.

The PURPOSE of that comment to me is _____.

The PURPOSE of this thought about my body, capability, intelligence is _____.

Sarah Ingmanson

The PURPOSE of my life is _____.

ACCEPT

From happen-*ing* to happen-*ed*... ACCEPT

"Pain is inevitable, suffering is optional", the saying goes. To opt out of suffering, we must accept.

Accept it. It happened... that's happen with an *-ed*. Those final two letters are critical as they signal past tense. Our suffering persists when we confuse *-ed* for *-ing* and keep past pain alive as present suffering. The past can only be happen*ing* if we allow it into our mind-space as a recurring nightmare. By recognizing the *-ed*, we can erase the hurt, the sting, the bitterness... and move past it.... before "it" takes root and transforms into resentment, apathy, or tolerance.

Resentment is anger. Apathy is numbness. Tolerance invites abuse. None of the above are acceptable!

Acceptance, on the other hand, breeds happiness. So, accept the very thing that riles you up. That gets your blood boiling. That saddens your heart. That causes you to toss and turn at night. Accept it. Why? Because it's holding you back. It's keeping you stuck where you never intended to be.

"I didn't know you were going through that at that time. You looked so happy."

I smiled to myself at the comment and thought back... yes, I was happy... happy in spite of the seeming turmoil around me. Happy because it was my first taste of freedom… and freedom always tastes good no matter how much it costs.

You see, once you accept an unexpected reality, you start to notice the unexpected blessings of the predicament. When you let go of how things were "supposed to" go, you see them without shades of judgment or emotional attachment to a specific outcome. With clarity of consciousness, you find beauty everywhere and invite peace into your soul.

Take an eraser to the scenario you had been visualizing and release it into the ether because everything appears differently through the lens of acceptance. Create distance… physically or just mentally. You are complete on your own and ready to live. The only person you need to stop being unfaithful to is yourself.

Accept yourself. There is nothing more comforting to your soul than this. Your true self. The self you are when no one is looking. The self you are when you stop judging yourself as incomplete. The self that shouts hurray when you decide to do something bold and defiant to realign yourself to your purpose and innermost desires.

So, let's accept what happened and dissolve happenings into something that happened… in the past… ridding our bodies of unneeded baggage, toxins, and internal conflict.

Word of the Week

ACCEPT a poor test result, outcome, illness, or letdown... as an opportunity to re-frame a belief, to reposition or to otherwise strengthen yourself.

ACCEPT a traffic jam, a delay, a snowstorm... or any other natural or man-made obstruction as a reminder to slow down.

ACCEPT a new role, job, or position that takes you closer to a life-changing dream, goal, or passion.

ACCEPT an offer of help... you are not meant to struggle alone or sacrifice your well-being.

ACCEPT love… especially love from yourself.

ACCEPT silence into the mind so the heart can be felt. When the mind is dominant, all emotion stems from thoughts and the day-to-day whims of your outside world.

ACCEPT the freedom to move, think, and feel for yourself without the coloring of other people's perspectives or past experiences. What is true for someone else doesn't have to be true for you… unless you *accept* that!

Word of the Week

ACCEPT people for who they are... not who you would like them to be... and navigate accordingly!

ACCEPT your age... as an achievement rather than a disappointment.

ACCEPT what resonates in you as a clue from your soul to pursue or explore.

EMOTION

Unlock your heart... EMOTION

Our shoulders tense up, our eyes well up, our stomachs turn in knots, our throats tighten, our fists clench, our hearts pound, we shiver from the chill of... voices rising, laughter erupting, sobs releasing. We hide them, succumb to them, react to them, try to out-think them, stomp around because of them... but, we cannot survive without them. So, we decide to thrive when we befriend them.

We reveal our inner world... our vulnerability... to the outer world when we share a moment through our eyes, our touch, our voice... and express our emotion.

Emotions comprise our personal navigation system... the source of our greatest intelligence... our inner intelligence and the connection to our higher self. Do you ever *feel* before you even *know* why or how or what for? Yes, we often know intuitively before we know cognitively. Our emotions are a barometer for how we're doing... right now. They issue warnings, affirmations, encouragement, and directions... where to go next. What needs healing. What needs contemplation. What needs feeling.

Emotions can overwhelm us and they can also entice us into suffering along with others. But, compassion does not entail suffering. Remember that. We lift and help others the most when we open our hearts without losing our center. Getting carried away by the same storm doubles the casualties. Instead, reach out a helping hand while standing on solid ground... centered within your heart space.

To stand strongly in emotion, you need to activate the willPower from your heart center.

Warm your body.

Indulge in a hot stone massage therapy and get literally warm to the bone. Pour a mug of your favorite hot beverage—green tea, hot cider, cocoa, coffee, or herbal tea... watch the toppings, watch the sugar count! Make a batch of chili healthily with plenty of veggies and extra lean ground turkey. Prepare a bubble bath with scented candles and a glass of wine (optional, but highly recommended!)

Eat "green" to balance your heart chakra with your warrior.

A healthy heart chakra vibrates at a frequency similar to the color green. Think outside the lettuce mix with avocados, limes, soybeans, green tea, basil, parsley. Vegetables provide the body with what it needs to feel grounded and yet expansive and loving. Especially effective are cruciferous veggies, such as broccoli, cauliflower and Brussels sprouts.

Pour passion into whatever you do this week.

Extend your arm a little more fully when you reach... or your eye contact when you articulate your opinion. Don't go through the motion. *Be* the motion. I know it's vague, but I want you to figure out what that motion is in your life. Your inner lover thrives on movement that is connected to your feeling.

Bonus: Buy (or accept... hint!) the gift of lingerie.

Allow it to symbolize your birthright to feel sexy, beautiful... and worthy of your desires. Find a store that honors your body and fits your personal style. Carve out the private space of intimacy where only one other sees you and knows this side of your beauty.

Strengthen the core of who you are [love] via heart-to-heart plank.

To practice, walk out to plank on the floor. Create a heart between your thumbs and index fingers below your "true" heart. Dedicate your plank practice to something you love about yourself or something you wish to express more fully today.

Advanced options: single leg lift, tricep push-up... leg lift + push-up!

Strengthen your heart muscle with blood-pumping cardio.

Get creative. Cardio need not be the treadmill... but it does need to get your heart rate up. Moving and shaking may be good for your inner artist (see next), but it will do nothing for your waistline if you don't get a little breathless. Invest in a heart rate monitor for a better "read" on the situation.

Open your heart through yoga "heart openers".

Try Camel Pose. The camel is a strong animal, representing the ability to accomplish the impossible and to go through life's challenges with ease. If you feel disconnected from the world, your family, or certain relationships, or are struggling with forgiveness, practice camel pose to help you express your feelings and find compassion towards others.

To enhance the exercise, think of something that no longer serves you—whether it's a thought pattern, habit, relationship, or situation in your life. As you anchor down through your lower body, lift up through your upper body, and let go of the fear that backward bending can hold. Release it, all of it. Let it go. Never to return.

Tune in your heart strings by dancing, singing, or listening to music that touches your heart.

Music ignites our creativity. Dancing is a fun way to tap into your self-expression and to get the creative juices flowing. Did you know that dancing has an effect on the body similar to meditation? Bust a move and bring out your inner muse!

Color coordinate with the heart.

Rock the red manicure or pedicure, throw some pink roses in a vase, and enjoy the *midori* (Japanese for "greenery") if it's not snow-covered!

Word of the Week

Allow your heart to soar with the night.

"Let yourself get carried away by the night from time to time. Look up at the stars and try to get drunk on the sense of infinity. The night, with all its charms, is also a path to enlightenment." ~Paulo Coelho

HOPE

What it means to… HOPE

Instead of closing my Friday afternoon emails with "I hope you have a good weekend", I would instruct my colleagues to *have* one. To my friend going through a rough time, I don't hope things work out… I offer you my conviction that they *will*. But, as I look up the definition of *hope*, I realize that this is exactly what hope was intended to capture:

HOPE *(excerpt from dictionary.com)*

[n] a feeling that what is wanted can be had or that events will turn out for the best

[v] to look forward to with desire and reasonable confidence

Have we lost a little "hope" within the true essence of hope? When you hear, "I hope this comes through…", can't you feel the other person's doubt, their lack of conviction… the sense that the stars must align, a divine lottery must be won in order for things to actually come through? It seems "hopefully" could just as easily be replaced with "doubtfully".

But, hope is not doubt. And, hope should not be discarded. It should be revered as essential to life-giving endeavors and personal transformation. Hope is what turns hard work into joyous work. The mundane into the meaningful. Drudgery into inspired action.

Hope aligns you to your finest acts of life.

Word of the Week

"It's all about the journey" reveals the gift of hope. The act of going for something brings you closer to knowing yourself. It elicits growth and transformation from within the process... not from the outcome of the process. In the process of training for a race, writing a manuscript, or working toward a goal, we discover who we are and what we are made of.

Outcomes are over-glorified. Losing the game could be even better than winning it. Have you ever experienced that?

All outcomes provide feedback and guidance, not permanent glory and distinction. Sure, a win feels good... extremely good. And when we win, we should savor, recover, celebrate, and bask in the glow. But, it is the inspiration that follows, which matters more. The inspiration that nudges us ahead to the next event... or the inspiration that points us to new things.

Absent hope, we stop going for things. We don't see the point. We are more confident in our failure than in our success... or more pointedly, that there is no benefit in the "going for". We have given up before we have even reached the starting gate.

Hope and self-worth are intertwined. We do not become worthy through struggle. We already are. And, from there, hope is natural. True hope. Looking-forward-to-with-desire-and-reasonable-confidence hope. Define 'reasonable'. Yes, you get to define it. That's subjective. That's up to you. What is reasonable in your world? With hope as your companion in life, you continuously get to expand upon what is "reasonable".

"Your playing small does not serve the world." ~Marianne Williamson

Transformation is possible because free will exists. Every day, we have the option to choose... how to engage... whether to dwell on a life-taking thought pattern or to reach for a life-giving one. We are free to choose a new direction... a new way of being... a new way of looking at our situations or surroundings or... ourselves in the mirror. Take a new breath... with hope.

Before you begin, align your body with hope. Get off the soapbox of proving worthiness through struggle. Hard work for the sake of struggle will damage you… and everyone around you. It creates disease and contagion. Instead, seek ways to spark the creativity and disciplined effort from joyful sources.

Create momentum.

Each time you choose, see what feels best. Be playful with it. When you create something you don't want, smile and say thank you… thank you for showing me what I don't want. Then, back it up and choose differently next time. This is how we create positive momentum… from a place of empowerment, worthiness… and hope.

If it's freaking you out, you're not ready yet. You're getting ahead of yourself. Back up until there is no worry or doubt intermingled with your hope.

Word of the Week

Find the feeling first.

If you are waiting for the test result or desired outcome in order to "feel good", don't be surprised if it stays out of reach. Results flow from an emotional trail. Our only job is to find the good-feeling place aligned with our dreams and desires.

Bring to mind a current situation or area in your life where things come easily.

Acknowledge how your hope is not lacking here and you can easily see yourself successful in said endeavor. Don't overthink it. In my world, it is teaching fitness. In your world, it could be baking bread. When you're about to do something outside of your comfort level, bring this vision to mind to strengthen your resolve and balance your perspective.

Evoke the conspiracy theory from others.

People will mirror back what you're putting out. There is always internal work that must be done, that others can't see, that only you can feel. In your worry, though, others cannot give you anything other than something that matches your worry. In real time, they are reflecting what you're feeling. Find a way to feel something different that they can reflect.

Focus on the improvement in the way you feel, rather than the ulterior motive to get what you want. Haven't you ever thought you knew exactly what you wanted, only to discover something better? From this standpoint, hope becomes easy… because you trust in the unfolding no matter what the outcome.

Word of the Week

Become a genius.

Genius is just attention to a subject. You can be a genius at chaos... or you can be a genius at life-giving things. We become what we repeatedly do... and think. Live out your desires through practiced thought, action... and rest.

Find hope in the beauty and ease of the sunset.

Take a moment just to acknowledge the day... and any challenges from your day... with ease and compassion for yourself. Then,

Sarah Ingmanson

celebrate your victories… that is, places where things flowed easily… and supported your vision for how life should be.

Find acts of hope all around you.

At a wedding. In a pregnant woman's caress of her belly. In viewing a sporting event on TV. At your child's piano recital or school play. How many acts of hope can you find? For the more you notice hope, the more hope will show up in your life.

SEARCH

Time for a tune-up... SEARCH

How many times a week... a day... do you use search? Don't make me admit... it's almost embarrassing. And, I mean all the way from the life-saving, helpful, and practical... to the purely entertaining. More often, though, we are looking for solutions to problems... however big or small.

But, that can be the problem itself. We get in the habit of searching outside of ourselves even on the occasions when the solutions can only be discovered within.

Or, we keep some things away simply because we don't believe we'll ever find them. We think it will be a long difficult search for the "diamond in the rough". The real issue, though, is we feel we are simply not worthy of something so precious.

We do not always search intelligently either. Sometimes, we expand our search too far... other times, not far enough. And, when the search criteria is not refined, neither will be the search output. Garbage in, garbage out. Unless you are a baby, you would probably prefer to avoid sifting through the "garbage" and, instead, receive something custom-tailored to your desires.

A search engine is a man-made invention replicating a human function. Our innate guidance is divine. But, like any engine, our internal search engine requires the periodic tune-up.

Sarah Ingmanson

"The human brain is fascinating; we will forget a scent until we smell it again, we will erase a voice from our memory until we hear it again, and even emotions that seemed buried forever will be awakened when we return to the same place." ~Paulo Coelho

We have instincts that will lead us to where we need to go and to the parts of us that require attention or healing. We may need to shift our focus to view the whole picture. Or unearth buried emotions and let them go.

SEARCH for hunger.

We do not appreciate contentment without experiencing a hunger pang. Your hunger pang need not be merely physical hunger either. It is hunger as you define it… and as you feel it within yourself. Trust those hunger pangs as a sign you are approaching "E" and need to fuel up.

Search for contentment.

When you feel it, smile to yourself because you are in a great place. Then, recognize you won't stay here… and you weren't meant to. It is within our nature and our life purpose to keep expanding and reaching for new desires. You simply cannot stay content in one place. Energy is always moving. And you are energy.

Search for what you want vs. what you think you need.

"Going after a dream has a price. It may mean abandoning our habits, it may make us go through hardships, or it may lead us to disappointment, et cetera. But however costly it may be, it is never as high as the price people paid by people who didn't live. Because one day they will look back and hear their own heart say, 'I wasted life'." ~Paulo Coelho

SEARCH for unconditional love.

When you are in a "pleasing" mode with someone who does not love you unconditionally, you are motivated to different behavior... with feelings of guilt, blame, resentment, and possibly powerlessness. You are modifying your behavior in order to appease someone else. Your internal feeling always reveals when this is happening. Search for it.

SEARCH the inner dialogue.

Actively replace judgmental or critical thoughts (of self or others) with compassionate or at least curious ones. Something that really charges you up... stop and take a step back with the words, "Hmm, that's interesting." Act as if you are watching the movie, not starring in it. Notice how the charge dissipates when you're no longer connected to it so directly or emotionally.

SEARCH for answers... honoring what is true for you.

Trust the feeling of knowing your truth. If it feels harmonious, fun, and freeing, give yourself permission to fly. Ignore whatever may be true for others if it doesn't trigger resonance within you. Embrace your creativity as in your power to create your world and your life experience.

Word of the Week

SEARCH for signs.

Indicators. Clues. Guidance. Evidence. They are all around when you open your eyes to them.

SEARCH for the right words to express yourself.

Words have long-lasting power. Think back. I bet you can remember something poignant that someone said to you as a child… that had long-lasting benefit (or detriment).

Sarah Ingmanson

SEARCH yourself... with curiosity to know, uncover, and create peace.

Meditate. See what surfaces. There is a reason we are called human *beings,* and not human-*doings.*

SEARCH for the purpose... the point... the lesson.

Don't hold yourself to perfection. Hold yourself to evolving.

"Every experience, no matter how bad it seems, holds within it a blessing of some kind. The goal is to find it." ~Buddha

SEARCH the edges. Search for deeper meaning. Go beyond what is said. Search for guidance, search for answers, search for clues, search for the truth. Search within the noise, yourself, the conversation. Go one level deeper. And, above all, take responsibility for how you feel.

INSPIRE

Pssst, over here... INSPIRE

When you feel a pang of inspiration, consider it a divine clue. A clue toward a latent talent, a key ingredient to your purpose... a signpost beckoning you, "Psst, over here!"

"Whatever inspires you is an aspect of yourself. Any desire of the heart exists to support you in discovering and manifesting it." ~Debbie Ford

So, roll up your sleeves and get motivated! No, wait, don't. Motivation entails nose-to-the-grindstone, hard work in a no-mercy, action-oriented kind of way. Inspiration is the reverse. Inspiration takes hold of us and directs us toward our desires.

Inspiration happens when we allow ourselves to be moved by a force that's more powerful than our ego. We recognize it by how it feels inside. Insistent. Encouraging. A small voice urging us toward stage, toward some far-off destination, toward another. Seemingly nonsensical even, we find ourselves saying, "Yes"... because saying, "No" is downright painful!

When we ignore inspiration, we trigger personal discomfort and create a disconnection within ourselves. We've resisted the calling to follow our path. We wander off aimlessly instead and try to block our ears to the voice... a voice that reminds us that this life experience is supposed to have meaning. This is the voice of inspiration. Ignore it at your folly.

Sarah Ingmanson

"For any number of reasons we might be resistant when we feel called to create, perform, visit a foreign place, meet someone, express ourselves, help another, or be a part of a cause. Inspiration is a calling to proceed even though we're unsure of goals or achievements—it may even insist that we go in the direction of uncharted territory." ~Wayne Dyer

To inspire literally means *to fill*... to fill others, your lungs, yourself... *with the urge or ability to do or feel something.* Therefore, inspire does not involve deflating, depressing, or demeaning (others... your lungs... or yourself). The ego entices us to separate, to stand apart and say, "Look at me", but inspiration never separates; it is the liquid gold that unites us and lights up a path to a destination for others to access... through our shining example. Keyword: *shining*. When we are focused on what inspires us, we feel no need to impress, outshine, or belittle anyone else. We are "on" in the best sense of the word—in-spirit, joyful, and drawn to our personal horticultural masterpiece.

"We're all assigned a piece of the garden, a corner of the universe that is ours to transform." ~Marianne Williamson

There are times, though, when we feel utterly uninspired and need to reconnect ourselves, clear the cobwebs, part the clouds, and cleanse our spirit to receive these divine messages.

See your rawness as the spark it is.

Word of the Week

Your rawness is where you are rough around the edges. The key is to allow these raw feelings inspire you into action. Find the opening... the soft spot in your heart that breaks through the walls and barriers you have built from experiences of pain and feelings of fear.

"We train in freeing ourselves from the tyranny of our own reactivity, our own survival mechanisms, our own propensities to be hooked." ~Pema Chodron

Create inspirational space... in your body.

Tight hips affect everything from our ability to lunge to being able to pick something up off the floor. Opening the hips reduces the load and overuse of the spine. It also creates an energetic shift. Hips are believed to be a storage ground for negative feelings and pent-up emotions, especially ones related to control in our lives. Hip-opening creates space for the birth of new ideas and new pathways, access to freedom in the body and in our own unique expression—creatively, physically, sexually, and spiritually.

Find solace in self-care.

When you feel disconnected to your physical body, it's time to stop, drop, and listen. Rest and nurture yourself. Eat grounding foods, with emphasis on high-quality carbs and proteins. Things like oats, sweet potatoes, bison, hummus, protein pancakes. Foods that give you energy and strength while honoring your commitment to a healthy body.

Stop wasting your time on the defensive.

"For the warrior, there is no 'better' or 'worse': everyone has the necessary gifts for his particular path. But certain people insist. They provoke and offend and do everything they can to irritate him. At that point, his heart says: 'Do not respond to these insults, they will not increase your abilities.' A warrior of light does not waste his time listening to provocations; he has a destiny to fulfill." ~Paulo Coelho

Take the vow to awaken so others can.

Word of the Week

Just as we recognize the importance of not self-denigrating with thoughts like, "I'll never get it" or "I'm a hopeless cause", there is shared responsibility to not denigrate others by criticizing their culture, traditions, or beliefs. Bias or bigotry stops inspiration dead in its tracks because you are fixating on things that are not at all "in-spirit".

"If your mind is expansive and unfettered, you will find yourself in a more accommodating world, a place that is endlessly interesting and alive. Genuine freedom comes from going beyond labels and projections, beyond bias and prejudice, and taking care of each other." ~Pema Chodron

Speak Beautiful.

Dove+Twitter: #SpeakBeautiful

Last year women sent over 5 million negative Tweets about beauty and body image. But it only takes one positive Tweet to start a trend.

Watch what you say. Out loud and, especially, to yourself. When I'm teaching fitness classes, I observe body language to "hear" the self-talk... my goal is to make it more 'beautiful'. Because I know the body will follow. Find ways to speak beautiful while being authentic. Change your perspective to beautiful wherever... however much... you can.

speak beautiful → *align with* beautiful → *feel* beautiful → *inspire* beautiful

Forget what-is.

Focusing on undesirable elements of the present is like broadcasting the message, "More of this, please". When you don't like the song playing on the radio, do you keep listening or do you change the station? When the food on the plate is not what you ordered, do you eat it anyway? Why would you? Good question… keep asking yourself, 'why would I?'

When you feel that pull of inspiration, you envision yourself there… if only for a moment, you imagine. But, what comes next is critical. Do you block the inspirational flow with doubt, rationalization or fear of failure? Or, do you invite it in with the thought, "More of this, please."

When you love yourself, there is no doubt of your worthiness to receive. So, get yourself in the mood. Read an autobiography. Watch the documentary. Go to the show. Learn from. Be inspired by. Take steps in the direction of. Small steps. Symbolic steps. Maybe things only you know about.

Look outside yourself.

Nature is the most divine spark of inspiration. Think of the beauty of a sunset, the sound of waves crashing, the smell of pine trees intermingled with ocean air… the chirping of birds, the look in your dog's eye when you say, "Wanna go to the park?", the aroma of oatmeal raisin cookies in the oven… these sounds, sights, scents inspire us by soothing us to our most natural state and reminding us of who we are in the realm of things... lucky to be here.

"We are afraid to change because we think that, after much effort and sacrifice, we know our present world. And even though that world might not be the best of all worlds and even though we may not be entirely satisfied with it, at least it won't give us any nasty surprises. We won't go wrong. When necessary, we will make a few minor adjustments so that everything continues the same. And we say: 'We want to be like the mountains and the trees. Solid and respectable.' Even though, during the night, we wake up thinking: 'I wish I was like the birds, who can visit Damascus and Baghdad and come back whenever they want to.' What a a life! Nature is telling us: 'Change!' And we fear this call. Because we feel safe. But to those who believe that adventures are dangerous, I say, try routine: that kills you far more quickly." ~Paulo Coelho

Dream of dolphins... or better yet, Dolphin Plank!

Dolphins are inspirational creatures, reminding us to utilize our gifts to move forward. Dolphins symbolize intellect, mental attributes and emotional trust. Dolphins also represent our willingness to navigate through emotional waters. To clear the third-eye chakra governing intuition, try this variation of plank.

With your elbows on the floor directly under your shoulders, bring your hands into prayer. With strong legs and an engaged belly, think about expanding your lower back. Now, imagine that your prayer hands and the third eye are connected by your intention. Keep your focus here for 5-10 breaths.

Connect others to a higher purpose. Encourage vulnerability, diversity, and fresh ideas to elicit others' talents, commitment, and dedication.

"Effective leaders develop a sense of purpose by pursuing goals that align with their personal values and advance the collective good. This allows them to look beyond the status quo to what is possible and gives them a compelling reason to take action despite personal fears and insecurities. Such leaders are seen as authentic and trustworthy because they are willing to take risks in the service of shared goals. By connecting others to a larger purpose, they inspire commitment, boost resolve, and help colleagues find deeper meaning in their work." ~ Ibarra, Herminia, Robin J. Ely, Deborah M. Kolb ("Women Rising: The Unseen Barriers", *Harvard Business Review*, Sept 2013)

LISTEN

Baby, I was born this way... LISTEN

"I was born this way." The perfect explanation when someone questions your greatness, quirkiness, belief system, or some facet of your journey here. You were put on the spot, so you need to respond, but there is no point in explaining... unless the other person is listening. And, by listening, I mean, wanting to hear.

Can't you feel when another is not really listening or not interested in your answer? It's uncomfortable. And, beyond not wishing to trigger that discomfort in another, we wish to avoid shallow life-dulling experiences. To sharpen our life, we must first sharpen our listening skills.

Listening is intelligence. Building awareness. A tool to strengthen. A secret weapon in a world infiltrated with noise and self-absorption. When we recognize that our outer world brings us clues and guidance, we recognize the importance of listening.

When another speaks, do you catch yourself thinking of something you want to say? It's natural. It's also impulsive. Conversations with my mom. We both have lists... mine in my head, hers on a piece of paper. Or, something a new acquaintance says reminds you of a personal experience. So you share it. It's relationship-building to search for common ground. But, it's dangerous if we don't keep our propensity to talk in-check and balanced with our willingness to listen.

Sarah Ingmanson

"We have two ears and one mouth and we should use them proportionally."
~Susan Cain

Learned experience becomes bodily wisdom. We have to condition the body so there is wisdom to listen to. Then, we train the mind to listen to the body. Close the loop.

"Genes are physical memories of an organism's learned experience." ~Bruce Lipton

Cue this week's audibles and become an expert listener:

LISTEN as you become one with the situation. Right action always emerges from that space.

"Satori is a moment of Presence, a brief stepping out of the voice in your head, the thought processes, and their reflection in the body as emotion." ~Eckhart Tolle

Word of the Week

LISTEN for the beat, the chorus, the crescendo.

Life is better when you move to a beat… obviously, thinks your inner dancer. We develop our ear when we listen for the nuances in the music. It helps us recognize and soar with the crescendos in our own lives.

LISTEN during moments of personal turmoil or crisis.

"Underneath all that we are taught, there is a voice that calls to us beyond what is reasonable, and in listening to that flicker of spirit, we often find deep healing." ~Mark Nepo

LISTEN with alertness, stillness, and presence.

Be there for another's benefit and watch what opens up in your world, in your body, in your heart.

LISTEN to the wholeness of the orchestra… or the person standing in front of you.

"The music is not in the notes, but in the silence between." ~Mozart

LISTEN to your self-talk.

Do you have a "sad story" you keep repeating? What are you creating with it? Does realizing this inspire you to speak differently? Lose the story and… gain a life!

LISTEN for inner cues and warnings.

The artist in you knows that listening is more art than science. And, at times, the goal isn't to get the perfect play, it's to get out of a bad play.

Word of the Week

LISTEN to the traffic... the background noise... the wind... the rainfall... the birds.

Notice how your obsessive thoughts about past or future melt away when you anchor to the simplicity and beauty of the present.

LISTEN for messages urging you here, guiding you there.

"They can come from the lips of a stranger we suddenly and mysteriously encounter at just the right instant. If we listen carefully, we always hear the right words, at the right time, to dazzle us into a realization of something that we may have failed to notice only moments before." ~Gregg Braden

LISTEN to your higher self and cut off your ego.

How do you know "which one" is talking? Easy. The higher self is the voice that is always patiently encouraging... always in your corner... yes, listen to that one. Hint: you might need to meditate and eliminate the noise to hear her.

LISTEN to your soul... it is whispering something to you... right now.

TRUST

Dare to... TRUST (again)

Once bitten, twice shy. Like wounded birds who fell out of our nests, do we dare to fly again? Oh... but what is the alternative? To never trust anyone, anything, any possibility again? To close shop and look upon the world with suspicious eyes?

Fact: we all face this temptation at some points in our lives. But, without trust, we screw ourselves over. We poison our soul and harden our hearts. We find more things to blame than to be grateful for. Our capacity to love becomes threatened by our propensity to fear. When we don't trust, we shut ourselves off from the ecstasies of life.

Trust is the glue that puts us back together. Trust opens us up to experience the orgasmic highs of life. Trust lifts our spirit, our posture, our eyes... to growth, expansion, and joy... to life at its most amazing.

"It is only trust that enables us to roam through the world, one foot nailed to the ground, attached to the string that will lead us back to where we've come from." ~Joan Chittister

When we shift our so-called trust issues onto others, we miss the point. Distrust of others reflects an inner distrust of self. How can this be? *They* did it, we think. *They* betrayed us... or life betrayed us. Neither is true. Betrayal is an inner state of confusion. Life will show you over and over again you have no authority to be in control of anything but one thing: *yourself.*

Word of the Week

"For peace of mind, resign as general manager of the universe." ~Larry Eisenberg

Self-control is vitally important to willPower. All other types of control show a lack of trust. A lack of trust in the unfolding of life. To replenish your innate reservoir of trust, grab your bucket... and start bailing... water, not your soul.

TRUST your feet.

Your feet are your connection to the earth. You can only trust these puppies if they are strong *and* pampered. Barefoot classes, lifting all ten toes up and down as you wash dishes, practicing soft landings as you walk, leap, or jump... foot reflexology, sugar scrub, pedicures... Feet are at the base of the kinetic chain that keeps you standing. Hip or knee problems often stem from here. Take care of your feet or they will take care of you!

TRUST the process... of elimination.

Reduce your cable bill, clear out old clothes. Often, the process of elimination is cleansing. At other times, it feels downright scary. We cling to things thinking they make us secure, but the irony is, the more we accumulate, the more measures we have to take to keep all of our stuff secure. And, nothing is really secure. So, it's when we finally release our false sense of security, we gain true security. And with security, comes trust.

TRUST your triggers.

Things that trigger you are nothing to be ashamed of. They represent places where you've been wounded and now beckon you to introspect, to peel away a layer of hurt, and to, above all, 'fess up in awareness that your reaction was an overreaction to the now, but reflective of some by-gone.

TRUST your gut.

The solar plexus chakra houses our willPower. When we are giving ourselves away or have become depleted in self-worth, we create blockages in the solar plexus, often experienced as stomach or digestive problems. Stomach in knots is literally true! When I am stressed, I could be confused for pregnant—my stomach bloats so much. As soon as the stress goes down, the belly goes down... and thus a fantastically easy (but to my ego, embarrassing...) way to monitor my stress or anxiety levels.

TRUST your coaches.

Be deferential to their expertise. Watch how it eliminates stress from your life and empowers them to do their thing. We don't like working for micro-managers, so don't be one either! Your accountant, your realtor, your investment advisor... your fitness instructor!

TRUST your heart.

Choose heart-centered responses and heart-centered action. When we lead from the heart, we do no real harm. Even if it's tough talk or bold action, staying heart-centered allows us to maintain healthy boundaries as we swim forward, setting up a positive wave for others in our divine ocean to surf.

TRUST the basic goodness of the person standing in front of you.

Trust the one who wants "in". Allow this person the chance to show up. Past hurts tempt us to close off before giving another a chance to show us what he or she is made of. The problem, of course, with that is...

"Every blessing ignored becomes a curse." ~Paulo Coelho

TRUST at the level of change.

Physical change is the most difficult to manifest because the energy is the densest in the physical plane. That's why it's critical to start at the level of thought and feeling... more accessible via meditation. Develop awareness for the narration you are layering onto your life situation. A distrustful person spins tragedies; a trusting person spins adventures.

TRUST in perfect timing.

Catch yourself when you think something isn't coming through fast enough... or, it wasn't supposed to happen so soon... or, at all! Your annoyance with timing reminds you of your place in life. Respond to the unfolding of events with the calm trust in perfect timing...

because things always work out in your favor... when you stop attempting to orchestrate.

TRUST it's not happening to you, it's happening for you.

This is difficult at times to accept because we have such limited view. Over time, we will see the perfection. When my father died during my junior year of high school, I lamented how unfair. But, I started to see the utter perfection in my life unfolding. How his death set off a series of events, changed perspective, and intense conviction... molding me into the woman I am today. A friend once told me, "It's a gift to have a loved one on the other side." I firmly know this to be true. Anyone who has experienced this can attest. They are with us always.

TRUST we are born to die. Live an adventure instead of a tragedy. Dare to trust... again.

CLARITY

"Land ho!"... CLARITY

From the air, the clouds break, and you catch the first glimpse of land. Ahhh... home soon. Or new adventure begins. Or a big meeting looms closer. Clarity strikes when land appears.

Clarity is seeing the writing on the wall... perhaps, *finally* seeing the writing on the wall. For a while, you were too far away, so you couldn't make out the words. Maybe you guessed or attempted to orchestrate the desired outcome, only to (re)discover that uninformed action leads to back-peddling and frustration. Hopefully, you used your willPower to trust that the answers would arrive in perfect timing.

The Universe speaks to us in ways we will understand. Before clarity arrives, there are little hints prodding us along. Nudging us this way, not that. Then, when clarity hits, we see the full picture—the beauty of the panoramic view... or the shock of the panoramic view! Realize we were never meant to suffer. We suffer when we resist or try to alter what clarity is revealing to us.

During TRUST week, it may have felt like you were stuck in a holding pattern. In a flash, the red lights all turn green and, with CLARITY, now you can cruise toward your destination. Or, you realize that the oasis you thought you were in is actually a large sink hole. Get out fast! Clarity brings realization, information, and understanding.

Clarity is an *aha* moment. Clarity is freedom from indistinctness or ambiguity. In other words, we now know what we're dealing with.

Or, we feel clear (clear*er*...) on action... which step(s) to take next. Recent clues piece together like a puzzle and we start to see how they fit... and what they form... so, we may fit and form.

Clarity is one of the Four C's used to calculate the quality and value of a diamond. Cut, color, carat, and... clarity. Clarity in diamond terms is the presence (or absence) of tiny imperfections called inclusions within the stone or on the surface of a stone. Higher clarity is rarer in nature. Diamonds come out of the ground with imperfections. Many inclusions, however, are not visible to the naked eye. So, we need magnification to detect them... in diamonds... and in ourselves.

Try inversion.

When the head is below the heart, gravity provides the brain with more oxygen and blood thus increasing mental function, and improving concentration, memory, and... clarity.

Take out time to rest, relax… and play.

"Every now and then go away, have a little relaxation, for when you come back to your work your judgment will be surer. Go some distance away because then the work appears smaller and more of it can be taken in at a glance and a lack of harmony and proportion is more readily seen." ~ Leonardo da Vinci

Pause and exhale.

Clarity can be overwhelming. Take time to adjust to your new surroundings, time zone, language, or other form of reality.

Move the body… regularly… repeatedly… in life-enhancing ways.

Word of the Week

Stretch, dance, lunge side to side. Your body was meant to move. Become a good mover. Today.

Be compassionate with yourself and others involved in your clarity.

In this world, we are tempted to classify events as ones we have "won" or "lost". That is the game of the ego. Rise above the ego's enticement and take a neutral view. Through neutrality, we "win" peace in our predicament.

Fill your heart with gratitude.

Gratitude for clarity… even if it's not what you wished for or expected. There is value in knowing, in knowing what to do next… in breaking the spell of denial… feel that.

"Denial, the act of not being aware of inner feelings and fears and motivations, is the opposite of mindfulness." ~Brian Weiss

Sarah Ingmanson

Listen to music.

Find clues directed to you from within the lyrics.

Meditate, journal, reflect.

Notice how your vision sharpens after meditation or periods of reflection. Clarity of thought brings clarity of vision.

Step back to look at the big picture.

We lose clarity when we overemphasize one event or area of our lives. Step back to see the entire picture of your life and the proper value or attention for this particular unfolding.

Above all, evoke the lessons of clarity.

We are never being punished by why happens to us, but there are always things to take with us… opportunities to integrate intuition with experience. In our lifetime, we often set out to evolve along certain dimensions… things like self-worth, faith, forgiveness, non-violence. Recognize that the clarity you experience this week is part of that evolving. What we don't learn this week, we will repeat.

"Why, if it was an illusion, not praise the catastrophe, whatever it was, that destroyed illusion and put truth in its place?" ~ Virginia Woolf

IF

Stretch assignment... IF

If x, then y... as in, y is conditional on x. For y to happen, x must. But for x to happen, *you* must happen. That is, you must entertain the thought, let desire pull you, energize what inspires you... with a powerful IF-statement.

When we start a sentence or a thought with a forward-looking "if" (especially in the form of "What if..." or "I wonder if..."), we create space for creativity, ideas, and inspiration to flow toward us. By looking at multiple "if's" (a.k.a. scenario planning), we get a handle on how sensitive our assumptions are to the predicted outcome. Scenarios expand our thinking and avoid a false sense of certainty in a single forecast. Scenarios are not foolproof, but they do help us ask better questions and figure out which drivers matter most.

If-statements stretch us to live a soul-expansive desire.

Backward-looking "if's", on the other hand, harbor regret. They limit and ill-equip us by assuming the future will resemble the past... and that change can only occur slowly. Through deliberate attention, focus, and willPower, we raise our point of attraction to a subset of possibilities that backward-looking "if's" could never possibly entertain. Once we realize that change must first happen at the level of the mind, we stop looking to the past as our hard-set possibility frontier and end the tragedy of the backward-looking "if".

Word of the Week

Stretching the mind beyond what we can see or quantify... feels uncertain, reckless... even dangerous. So, we stay tightly bound within our mind's history... where we think we're safe. With the body, we fall into the same trap but for different reasons. We skip stretching as we hurry onto a bigger calorie-burning exercise or our next item on the day's agenda. However, stretching is fundamental to wellness in both the mind and the body.

This week, use "if" as your stretch assignment and become more flexible physically and mentally. Stretch your ideas before making a decision. Generate scenarios from a new angle. Stretch your heart to appreciate the other person's perspective. Stretch your body in training to split. Stretch your mind with the intention to move beyond your boundaries... in the direction of miracles.

"Dwell in possibility." ~Emily Dickinson

Fill in these blanks. Journal the "why" or any aha thoughts associated with your responses.

"If. 'If' always propelled my thoughts back to the present, because 'if' depended so much on keeping my wits about me. I couldn't properly sense things if I was distracted. 'If' demanded my full presence and participation in 'now.' 'If', as much as it scared me, also kept me sane." ~Ransom Riggs

IF I could change one thing about my appearance or physical body, I would change _____.

IF I could break one habit, it would be my tendency to _____.

IF I could travel to one place in the world, I would jump on a plane to visit _____.

IF I could have one super power, it would be _____.

IF money were not a consideration, I would pursue a livelihood (degree, career, pastime, etc.) in _____.

Word of the Week

IF my friends or colleagues were describing me, they would mention this positive aspect first and foremost _____.

IF I were an animal, I would be a(n) _____.

IF I were allowed only one call, I would want to hear _____'s voice. (alive or deceased)

Sarah Ingmanson

IF I could go out to lunch with one famous person (actor, athlete, artist, author, leader, etc.), I would choose _____ (alive or deceased).

IF I could go back in time, I would relive the year _____ .

CONFIDENCE

Lose the comparison and gain... CONFIDENCE

With confidence, we shine... reflect... illuminate a lifeline to another who sees danger where we see adventure; possibility in the so-called impossible. Confidence energizes... expands... encourages, and unites. Confidence comes from a place of peace within you.

"Confidence is the purity of action produced by a mind free of doubt." -Katty Kay & Claire Shipman, The Confidence Code

With confidence, we don't embellish who we are... because we're not trying to be better than others; we're trying to be authentic and true to ourselves. Being authentic requires following our heart into the wilderness... the wilderness where our deepest fears of loss and failure lie. Confidence reminds us there is too much to be gained in the going-for and putting-ourselves-out-there to fixate on the what-if's of losing. The real "winning" is in our opportunity to grow and release old patterns of thoughts, beliefs, and behavior that no longer (or never did...) serve us.

"People are afraid to pursue their most important dreams, because they feel that they don't deserve them, or that they'll be unable to achieve them." ~Paulo Coelho

With confidence, we lose the mask of insecurity and self-hatred… because confidence never flaunts, brags, shames, or separates. A better-than-thou cockiness is not only a disservice to others, it encourages your ego to chant, "you will never be enough". External validation cannot quell the ego; the only thing that can is you… and your confidence.

"Grandiosity is always a cover for despair." ~A Course In Miracles

So, with authenticity and humility, we cultivate our confidence… and set about our mission… to shine… no matter what.

CONFIDENCE doesn't dwell on defeats. The Warrior understands that reliving the past in your mind guarantees a sequel in real life. Form follows thought, so choose your thoughts carefully. Be mindful of your internal dialogue.

"We are born with only one obligation—to be completely who we are." ~Mark Nepo

Word of the Week

CONFIDENCE asks, "What would I do if no one was watching?" How would I act... dress... dance? The lover in you finds the safe space... relationship... career to do this.

CONFIDENCE dresses for the occasion. The lover in you appears when you feel good in your skin. Suit up to shine and express yourself, not to mask. Go for the glitter even if it means paying extra. You deserve it. Start walking the walk and become the vibrational match to that which you know in your heart you can... and deserve... to be.

CONFIDENCE doesn't hoard the spotlight. Your inner athlete shifts it by becoming the spotlight... the illumination itself... shining outward with the question, how can I be of service to the world?

CONFIDENCE goes one level deeper when the temptation to outshine surfaces. "Why is it important that I feel superior here?" it prods. "What is the real issue or fear?"

Keep an eye out for shallow ego desires that you can lovingly replace with authentic heart-centered desires. Questions like, "Why am I engaging in this and interested in the going for?" will keep you heart-centered. Seek to understand inner motives to prevent slippage and to nip in the bud anything that isn't soul-serving.

As an artist, you communicate your CONFIDENCE through your posture, body language, and clarity of voice. As you see your body for the miracle it is, you can shine from that place of self-love and compassion in all of your art forms and communication.

Use music… a personal play list or a "pump-up" song to ignite your CONFIDENCE.

Word of the Week

CONFIDENCE doesn't believe in luck. The wise sage in you understands attraction and takes credit for all manifestations of that attraction... the good, the bad, and the... instructive.

Clean energy... your energy. Clear your chakras before meditation, exhale fully to allow stale air to release. Correct imbalances in your nutrition and recovery. Listen to your body and your higher self to see where your CONFIDENCE is lacking physically and/or emotionally.

RISK

Throw the dice... RISK

I live in Vegas, and yet I never "throw the dice"... at least not in a casino or slot machine sense. But, I do gamble every day... we all do.

To gamble is to take risky action in the hope of a desired result. Even in inaction, we are throwing the dice and taking a risk. The risk of getting caught. The risk of losing ourselves. The risk of things changing. The risk of things staying the same... So, the right question isn't, "Do you gamble?" It is, "What are you gambling?" And, "Which risks are worthy of your willPower?" To mobilize our CONFIDENCE, we must become cognizant of RISK.

"Once we believe in ourselves we can risk curiosity, wonder, spontaneous delight, or any experience that reveals the human spirit. ~e. e. cummings

Summon your inner riskologist, please.

"Risk•ol•ogist (noun): A practitioner of smart risks who thrives in an uncertain world." ~Tyler Tervooren

Word of the Week

RISK discomfort (← → stagnation).

Life out of the comfort zone is where transformation occurs. In the "La-Z-Boy", our core muscles atrophy. In shoes, the muscles in our feet atrophy. In the mundane, our minds atrophy. So get up... kick off your shoes... and find ways to breathe new life into your body, mind, and spirit... every day.

"Everyone has a 'risk muscle.' You keep it in shape by trying new things. If you don't, it atrophies. Make a point of using it at least once a day." ~Roger von Oech

RISK bulking up (← → driving on empty).

Schedule some buffer time between meetings or appointments. Find time alone to recharge. Enjoy a meal that is neither measured nor weighed. Excessive "doing" or deprivation impairs our productivity, our creative energy, our hormonal balance. Build up your reserves with laughter, recovery, and nutrients.

RISK abandonment (← →pleasing).

How others respond to your success... is it the same when you fail? I have certain people in my life who rush in when they sense tragedy. I realize it is soothing to them. But, these drama kings and queens can hold us back from the life imagined. The life you imagined. Notice when you are defending or downplaying your dreams. Recognize the difference between caring criticism and a rigid code of beliefs.

RISK failure (← → regret).

Never knowing haunts us in our sleep. "What if I had..." "I wish I had..." Once we put failure in its proper place, we take risks more easily. Our self-worth is never impaired from failure; it is impaired from living small.

"Failure enables us to take risks as we grow until we find where we really fit, where we cannot only succeed, but also enjoy the challenges of life as well."
~Joan Chittister

Word of the Week

RISK pissing off some people (← → living someone else's life).

I don't want my daughter to be a "mini-me"… in the sense of equating success with how closely she resembles me. I want her to explore and find herself. When we know ourselves, we live accordingly. Without a sense of shame, disloyalty, or disrespect when we don't love everything others love. We shine for the world to see our unique brilliance at our deepest level of truth. And those who love us unconditionally will applaud that light when it shines.

RISK asking (← → assuming).

Recognize it is only in our heads that we are starring in the lead role of our personal screenplay. Our supporting actors are doing the same in their minds—playing lead. This is why when we assume that our needs, wants, aspirations are obvious to others, they often are not. And, that theory you have conjured up in your head is often far from the truth. Take the risk and ask for what you want or to simply ask why. Give space for others to respond. You might be surprised… in fact, I bet you will!

"The answer is always NO if you don't ask." ~Stacey Lei Krauss

RISK the illogical (← → ignorance).

Some of my best decisions made no sense at the time… except in that inner voice of knowing. When we trust ourselves, we do not ignore our desires and our intuition… we listen to the small voice inside. The one that says "just go" or "yes". We take risks that instinctively feel right.

"Risk, the willingness to accept an unknown future with open hands and happy heart, is the key to the adventures of the soul. Risk stretches us to discover the rest of ourselves—our creativity, our self-sufficiency, our courage. Without risk we live in a small world of small dreams and lost possibilities."
~Joan Chittister

RISK pain (← → denial).

Facing the truth can be painful, but putting off that truth in the form of denial prolongs and exacerbates the suffering. Search for the pockets of denial in your life or lifestyle… where your desperation has crept in to rationalize your behavior… where your values do not match up with your actions… or where your actions do not align with your dreams and desires.

RISK eye contact (← → a fake smile).

Being vulnerable is a quality that stems from trust and confidence. We admire it in others, but it scares us to express it. We can hide behind a fake smile, but we cannot fake our eyes... they are our windows to the soul. Use them effectively. Dare to create more meaningful connection. Dare to express your "crazy". The world loves it... and, actually, needs it.

RISK a career (← → a job).

Sarah Ingmanson

Living just for today is the difference between having a job and a career. A career is planned, cultivated, refined, and purposeful... a job is often the opposite. With a career, you make investments. Long-term investments like continuing education, networking, a retirement savings account, a gym membership. Investments today provide future options tomorrow. Think beyond the current paycheck and invest wisely for long-term returns and longevity in your "career".

"I am always doing that which I cannot do, in order that I may learn how to do it." ~Pablo Picasso

RISK the discomfort of change (← → reckless destruction).

Think about the risks you are taking in your daily life. Which ones are conscious, deliberate, inspired, will-Power-ful? Which ones are unconscious, externally motivated, harmful... or even reckless? Only you know the answers. Trust yourself to throw the dice in the right direction.

"Risk prods us on to become always the more of ourselves. It is the invitation to the casino of life." ~Joan Chittister

CHALLENGE

Create to break... CHALLENGE

Breaking a habit is more difficult than creating a new one... scientifically. To do so, we have to resist the impulse associated with an established synaptic pathway—you know, like the well-established synaptic pathway that leads me to the Keurig machine in the morning...

And, while many of our impulses are benign... or even beneficial... such as when we automatically fasten our seat belts before putting the car into reverse, others are not... and must be overcome to achieve our goals. Habit *destruction* is most effectively accomplished by parallel habit *construction*. This is life's way of asking, "Will you accept this challenge?" The challenge to change... or perhaps the challenge to return to your truest self.

This week, we construct to destruct... we create to break. Step up to the challenge. Your greatness... not your punishment... awaits.

"When any behavior or pattern is repeated enough, the synaptic pathways associated with that pattern get used to being accessed. As a result, it becomes easier for impulses to travel along those pathways, and the behavior seems 'natural'."
~Julia Layton

Is it a lack of discipline or a lack of a synaptic pathway that keeps us from staying on-course? Depends. Do you prefer to feel guilty and ashamed... or compassionate and hopeful? We are what we repeatedly do. Repetition leads to results because it paves a well-traveled pathway... in your brain... from your heart. Your heart leads everything. It houses your desires. Conviction and rationalization from the brain follow.

If you've ever made a New Year's resolution, started a new diet, or tried quitting something, you know it's not the first week that's rough. It's the second or third week when the initial zeal wears off and resistance in the form of hunger, fatigue, and old patterns of behavior set in. This is why 21-day or 30-day challenges are so prevalent in fitness circles... they keep participants going after the inspiration has faded and when temptation strikes.

But, what happens after 3-4 weeks? The answer lies in you. Are you trying to make a short-term fix so you can go back to old patterns of behavior? Or, are you trying to make a change stick? Is the challenge-invoked behavior even worth sustaining or possible to sustain? If not, a good question might be... why bother? Are you impatient... in denial... or desperate? If we allow these emotions to run rampant, we become easy prey to deception in the fitness and weight loss industry. As practitioners or consumers of fitness, we have a responsibility and right to end the cycle wherever we can.

Understand the value in this. Once we're clear and confident in ourselves and our self-worth, we can acknowledge the risk(s) and accept (or reject) the challenge as an intelligent choice. Our intelligent choice. Sustained choice (a.k.a. change) requires adequate repetition plus desire. Desire to change. Are you ready for change? Then, please proceed...

To destruct a habit, we construct a parallel one. Parallel in feeling. A good meal or exercise plan takes what you like and "enhances" it with parallel improvements.

CHALLENGE the afternoon Starbucks.

If your energy levels are dropping in the afternoon, chances are you overdid it at lunch. Try splitting your lunch into two meals... one at noon and one at 3pm. More frequent eating is a principle of bodybuilding and an important way to regulate blood sugar. The key is to keep the portions small so as to not increase caloric consumption over the entire day.

CHALLENGE your grumpies. Before you reach for the Kleenex, seek solace in the form of daily meditation, yoga, creative activity (e.g. drawing, writing, gardening, dancing), a relaxing bath or massage, and adequate hydration. Start your day off on the right foot with a gratitude list. Minimum of 5. Effect amplified when written.

CHALLENGE your sweet tooth.

A 1/4 cup of berries, a tablespoon of cacao nibs, or a slice of cinnamon raisin Ezekiel bread can provide sweetness, texture, and flavor to your meal and help you overcome the impulse toward the bag of M&M's. Look for protein powder in your favorite sweet flavor, too.

CHALLENGE your metabolic furnace.

Beyond jalapeños, fasted steady-state cardio and/or (un-fasted) lifting sessions stoke hunger by lifting your metabolic rate via EPOC (Excess Post-exercise Oxygen Consumption, a.k.a. the "afterburn" effect). EPOC lifts your resting metabolic rate up to 36 hours after the session is over.

CHALLENGE the intensity of your workouts. Utilize super-sets, add heart rate-lifting exercises like push-ups, burpees, or jump lunges, and take stricter breaks between sets (e.g. 30-60 secs). Or, try a class that choreographs this in for you. My favorites are BodyPump and willPower & grace.

CHALLENGE overeating at night.

Often we fail to match our meals with our energetic output. We burn more calories in the morning after "fasting" overnight and when our activity level tends to be highest. By skipping breakfast or skimping out on protein, we set ourselves up for failure. As our energetic output wanes at night, we overload on calories either out of low intake all day, emotional craving, or simple habit. Balance out the meals better... or trick yourself with a large salad at night.

Tips to a healthy salad: Substitute high-fat or high-sugar "fat free" dressings with balsamic vinegar or apple cider vinegar. Use healthy fats such as avocado, extra virgin olive oil or flax oil... sparingly. Healthy fats are great for our skin and hair, and they quell the stomach growl effectively. Just go easy on serving size (e.g. no more than one tablespoon of oil or half of an avocado). Ground extra lean turkey, chicken breast, shrimp, and ahi tuna are excellent lean protein sources, while bison, salmon, and tofu are alternatives richer in Omega 3 fatty acids.

CHALLENGE the bag of popcorn or chips.

Try a spoonful of salsa on your lean protein-carb combo. Did you know that egg whites have more sodium than other sources of lean protein? And, a small portion of jalapeños delivers sodium in a form that lifts the metabolism.

CHALLENGE the apple, granola bar… or candy bar.

If you're a frequent flyer or just frequently on the go, don't pack snacks void of protein… protein is the one thing you "need" to preserve your lean muscle and to keep your resting metabolic rate intact. Pack a shaker with a scoop of protein powder. Add water and shake it up when needed. It will sustain you until your next meal.

CHALLENGE pizza… pasta or the food you have deemed "off-limits".

Make it healthier. Make it special. Make it strategic. A "good" or "bad" assignment is an unhealthy and limiting way of living. There are healthier ways to make virtually everything. Open your eyes to the ingredient list, portion size, and frequency.

CHALLENGE your mental muscle and plateaus.

Think long-term with goals, such as The willPower Method®'s World Plank or Hot by June (can you split?) seasonal challenges, a race, a contest, or any other measurable goal beyond the scale... and beyond 1-2 weeks. Our ability to achieve a goal and realize progress strengthens our confidence and fuels our motivation. Weight loss may be a pleasant side benefit, but our confidence gain needs to be the primary.

CONTROL

Don't make me lose it... CONTROL

"This is a story about control...", so summon your inner Janet. Or, better yet, summon your willPower... for willPower is a manifestation of control... self-control... the only true form of control available to you. Any other form of control is an insatiable and hopeless pursuit of the ego—to control the uncontrollable or to control things you were never meant to control. (FYI—this is what insurance is for...)

We have no control over places or spaces other than our own mental place or space. Don't let this dishearten you. Your control is a mighty force that magnetizes places and spaces to you, and is easily measured. If you're wondering how high you register on the control barometer, no need to search your food receipts or count the number of gym check-in's on your Facebook page, you simply need to check in with yourself and ask, "How am I feeling?"

"We call frustrating anything we want the world to confirm as justification for not being able to control the way we think." ~Joan Chittister

Next, take a look around. What kinds of places and spaces are you matching up to? The people and events that show up in your life are not the cause of your turmoil. Your mental garden is. Tend to it deliberately... with care. If a certain flower doesn't appeal to you... or causes you to sneeze, why do you keep planting it? Same with your thoughts. A destructive pattern of thinking will never yield anything different. Yet, we keep going there. Out of habit. Or out of an underestimation of the power of our will. Test it. Discover the correlation of what you put out there mentally to what you harvest physically in the garden of your reality.

Control is cultivated with self-awareness of our thoughts.

Self-awareness strengthens our control… control of thought to change neurological pathways and beliefs, and to release triggers, pent-up frustration, and past hurts. With control, we effect change from the inside out. For that is the only way to effect sustainable change.

Discipline is conventionally measured by our commitment to something outside of ourselves. We think that our tough action justifies our worth. Not ever. Repeat, not ever! We are worthy because we just are. So, ask yourself, what is making it impossible for me to accept the good of where I am right here right this minute? With control, we train our minds to resist the negative impulses within that keep us from experiencing the joy of life and the fullness of who we are. We slow down to grasp the true essence of what it means to be a human being. A healthy holy life is under our control… our mind's control. We are not a product of our environment. We are a product of our thoughts and our perceptions/distortions.

Control is a commitment to stop running from the truth of your life.

To experience your heart's desires, there is a path that must be undertaken. Along the path, there will be challenges. Control helps us follow the path of least resistance. We check in with ourselves continuously to stay on that path. We understand the risk of staying where we are. Halfway home is not home. We must keep going, but we seek our heart for the best route.

Control means taking responsibility for shaping our lives as life shapes us.

Control is our inner power. This inner power is non-threatening and connects us to others as universal collective energy. Worldly power entails the false hope of controlling things, people or situations.

It comes from a place of fear where control is used destructively. What does having a sense of external control do for you... require of you? Do you wish your legacy to be fearfully destructive or lovingly creative?

CONTROL your breath.

Breathe fully. When tense, just take a few deep breaths without doing anything else. Feel how it helps.

CONTROL your multitasking.

It's more difficult to stay aware and present when we are doing multiple things at once. We also use multi-tasking to distract ourselves from listening to or dealing with the thing(s) that really matter.

Word of the Week

CONTROL the guilt trip.

We are emotional beings. Control doesn't mean we hide our emotions or we get it right every time. Control means we learn from our experiences… with curiosity, compassion, and self-love.

CONTROL your fatigue.

Control is easier to have when rested. Fatigue shortens our fuse. Think beyond sleep, too. We rest when we savor a good meal or linger at one of our favorite activities.

CONTROL the power trip.

There is a way of standing in your power when you feel threatened or violated. This can mean not continuing a conversation that has no point except to attack or defend. Step outside it. Nothing can attack you unless you let it. Rewire your typical reaction to start a new pattern of behavior, to attract new opportunities… new ways of relating… new ways of being.

CONTROL the give and take.

We can't give, give, give (or take, take, take) without putting ourselves into disequilibrium. When you take on a new responsibility, release an existing one. When you buy new clothes, give away or donate something. Are you depleting yourself? Or putting yourself back together?

CONTROL the worrying

Worry is the mental echo of your fears. When we become consumed by the unknown, we lose our confidence and we bow down to fear.

Free yourself from worry and start living. Each step into the unknown builds our confidence. Reach out for others. Let their love nourish you instead of your fear.

"I will always have fears, but I need not be my fears for I have other places within myself from which to speak or act." ~Parker J. Palmer

CONTROL what you say, type, or express in your body language.

It's a personal responsibility. While we cannot control what others think, feel, act, or say, we can control our response to it. Take a moment to reflect, filter, pause, exhale... to choose differently if that feels right in your heart. Notice how often you dilute your positive statements with a "but..." or "if only".

CONTROL your momentum.

Catch yourself entering the tunnel of negativity. It's easier to stop momentum when we're closer to the light, then once our negativity has immersed us in the darkness.

CONTROL the labeling of yourself.

There are built-in limitations within the roles we play or cast others to play. Are you flowing downstream in the direction of what you want… really want… or upstream because of what somebody else is doing, or what you used to do, or what someone else thinks you should do? When you turn inward and adjust your thoughts to flow with your energy stream, you start getting control over your life.

BALANCE

Coming soon... BALANCE

Without balance, we fall or fail. With balance, we may wobble, but we regain our steadiness. Most critically, we stay standing. The knockout punch does not send us down. When we get dizzy, we find our eyes in the mirror. Examples of balance inspire us... examples such as the woman in front of me striking the perfect star pose in my yoga class... at 35 weeks pregnant.

I have a few members in my classes near-term in their third trimesters. Of course, I admire what they are doing for themselves and for their babies, but I love what they are doing for all of us in class. Pregnancy defies traditional logic. It is not injury or disease, it is gestation... incubation... God-gifted evolution. Hormones surge, creating glow, fatigue... and often nausea. A shine from the inside out... even if that entails one's lunch from the inside out.

At my first prenatal appointment, my doctor instructed me to lift no more than 15 lbs. When I pressed her for why, which body parts, and whether my existing muscle mass or past lifting experience factored into this precise number, she answered, "No, this is just the guideline for all pregnant women." I looked her in the eye incredulously waiting for her to waiver, but she returned to her clipboard for the next item on her checklist. I wasn't sure she had ever lifted a weight in her life, so I decided to let it go. I decided then that this pregnancy would be my own... when it came to fitness and nutrition. I would become the student of my pregnant body. I would trust it to tell me what I could do... and when I should stop. I would honor the baby growing inside to eat when (and what) she demanded (primarily, Subway, Chipotle, and Einstein's...), to know the difference between intensity and harm... intelligence and stubbornness... self-kindness and insanity.

"Nobody knows less about fitness and nutrition than your doctor." ~Michael Battaglia

Balance is nothing unique to pregnancy; pregnancy simply heightens it... and makes it easier. In any given endeavor, there is an ongoing balance we must find for ourselves... for our growth, our health, and our longevity... for our mind, body, and spirit. When there is a baby growing inside, it becomes easier to treat ourselves with kindness. Personal growth occurs when we do this while there is not.

"Six-pack Abs... Coming Soon!" her T-shirt read. I pointed and smiled as we were setting up for triceps in a BodyPump class. She nodded, "Key phrase, Coming Soon." She laughed and then added, "But, Sarah, I've been saying this my whole life!" Hmm, I thought, maybe that's the problem...

Are there things that you have been dangling in front of yourself as "Coming Soon" for months and months (or years and years)? Mentally, is there an element of "I will never have or reach this desired state" that is sabotaging your willPower? We need to find the right balance of intention and deliberate focus to realize our desires. We also need to sanity-check our desires... as we balance intensity and harm... intelligence and stubbornness... self-kindness and insanity.

Everyone has a six-pack... it is nothing you cultivate through abdominal exercise... it is revealed out of body fat. This is why it is so coveted; it is difficult to attain in one sex and unhealthy to attain in the other. It requires dropping body fat levels into the single digits. While most men can safely and naturally do this; most women cannot. Or, at least not without the use of drugs and/or posing health risks, such as amenorrhea, low bone density, hair loss, adrenal fatigue.

Word of the Week

Fortunately, most of us do not actually want a visible six-pack. We want a lean torso with some muscular definition. We want to feel good in and out of our clothes. We want to take care of our health because we know excess abdominal fat is the most detrimental. We want to stand confidently in our willPower because the midsection is typically the first place we accumulate fat and the last place we lose it. Therefore, it serves as a symbol… a personal symbol of our ability to balance.

In terms of body fat, there is a balance we must understand to unshroud the mystery and debunk the gimmicks. The balance between catabolism and anabolism… destroying and building… generating and consuming energy. So, this week, look at the following all together. These are ten succinct tips… tips that work… and need to be integrated into one lifestyle if lowering body fat has been "Coming Soon" for way too long.

BALANCE your insulin: eat right after awakening and right after lifting.

Insulin (a critical anabolic hormone) drops overnight as glycogen is depleted. Working out also depletes glycogen (energy) stores. Our bodies are breaking down fat… and muscle because our bodies are in a catabolic state. To stop the breakdown of muscle, it is important to eat right away. Just eating carbs… especially high Glycemic Index carbs (e.g. juice, white bread, most cereals or pastries)… spike insulin and encourage fat storage… while muscle continues to break down. See next.

BALANCE out all that sugar. No juice... or you might as well add vodka.

The most comparable thing to that glass of juice? Take a glass of water and dump a bunch of sugar into it. So, if you're going to opt for juice, might as well make it more enjoyable with a splash of vodka. Or, if you are serious about revealing your abs, always pair your fruit (preferably in raw or blended form...) with protein.

BALANCE your meals with protein in every single one.

No exceptions. Lean protein. Enough protein. 3-5 egg whites would be better than 1 egg. No skin on your chicken. Grab some scissors and trim the fat before cooking. Protein prevents catabolism of our most metabolically active tissue... muscle. See next.

BALANCE your metabolism. No crash diets.

Preserve your basal metabolic rate. A severe drop in calories triggers your body to alter its metabolism so that less energy is burned, while at the same time storing any energy it can find. Where are crash diets most prevalent? The US and the UK. Where are obesity rates the highest in the word? The US. In Europe, the UK.

BALANCE all those so-called "good" fats with realistic portions and frequency.

When leaning out on a crash diet or an extreme diet (e.g. broccoli and chicken), your skin tone will suffer devoid of proper nutrition. Healthy fats such as avocado, extra virgin olive oil, and almonds are great for glowing skin, healthy nails and hair. An avocado not only contains an impressive list of vitamins and nutrients, it enhances the absorption of nutrients in other things you are eating... such as the nutrients in your salad. An avocado is a fruit hefty in fat, so it also satiates our tummies when we're trying to reduce body fat. Just be cognizant of the 9 vs. 4 ratio. (Fat delivers 9 cals per gram; Carbs & proteins deliver 4). As a guideline, limit your intake to less than half an avocado or a tablespoon of olive oil or almond butter... in 1-2 meals per day.

BALANCE out your body. Lift legs to lose body fat.

In the Male Physique division of Bodybuilding, the lower body isn't even visible to the judges (thanks to board shorts), so it seems odd that these competitors would train legs... unless you understand the anabolic effect of lifting. Lifting the biggest muscle group in the body gets you more cut all over because you are lifting the anabolic hormones during the session, which stimulate protein synthesis and muscle growth.

Sarah Ingmanson

BALANCE through your core. Engage your abs… especially while lifting.

Make every lift an abdominal exercise. Brace your abs as you squat or dead lift, and engage core muscles to keep your body still and stable doing bench flies. Abdominal exercises, and the proper execution of hovers, planks, and push-ups especially, teach us how to brace the midsection, reminding us to engage them more throughout the day. Postpartum, heightening this awareness is key to retraining the midsection.

BALANCE your workout with appropriate sequencing. Never do cardio before lifting.

Cardio zaps your strength before you've even started lifting. Most likely, you are just getting into a fat-burning zone when you stop cardio (around 30 minutes) and start lifting. So, you are falling short in both endeavors. If you want to combine lifting and cardio, always do your cardio at the end.

Word of the Week

BALANCE your goals with sufficient time. Beyond 30 with aerobic.

Whether you are climbing stairs on the StairMaster, sprint/jogging intervals on the treadmill, cycling, dancing, kickboxing... or even BodyPump (due to the high rep nature, BodyPump has a high aerobic component), the 30 minute mark is generally where most of us start burning fat, so go for 45-60 minutes. Invest in a heart rate monitor (with chest strap) for more accuracy and accountability.

BALANCE the intensity with your overall workout time. Get to failure by 30.

If your *strength* training sessions, however, exceed 30-45 minutes, chances are you not training intensely (heavy) enough. To get the anabolic effect described for your Athlete, intensity is key.

BALANCE strength training and cardio with other classes or agility training, such as willPower & grace, yoga, Pilates, etc. You will not achieve as high a calorie burn, but you will strengthen your form, your mind-body connection, and your flexibility so you can achieve full range of motion with proper alignment… and a sunnier outlook! Always be meticulous with your form so that you can make intensity gains while avoiding injury.

STRENGTH

Past neuroticism... land softly in STRENGTH

When lifting, a still body helps you isolate the target muscle group... to train more effectively... to train more safely. You invite stillness into your body by bracing your core. You invite stillness into your mind by knowing your core... who you are at your core. The solar plexus chakra houses our ability to be confident and in control of our lives. It is affected by self-worth, self-confidence, self-esteem. Not coincidentally, it is located in your core. We develop both types of "core" through a commitment to a continuing education in... strength.

I appreciate soft landings... when I'm flying into Narita and when I'm jumping in class... soft landings improve the quality of my flight, my training session... and my life. Strength is not just about how high we can jump, it's also about how (or whether) we land on our feet. So, care about how you land.

Everything fires up from the floor... and your feet are the connection to that. If you are wearing something that performs the function of supporting your foot, the muscles in your feet forget how to... because they don't need to. You can perform the exercise without focusing on alignment and not get injured. Therein lies the tragedy.

There is nothing like a heavy weight to tell you when your form or alignment is off. You could have poor form with a light weight and stay free of injury forever... and also free of results... tragically. You can go long distances as a heel striker in traditional shoes or land heavy on your feet in ultra-supportive shoes... also staying free of injury... perhaps. Training barefoot or in minimalist shoes disallows this. It's not the shoes that are dangerous; it's the person wearing them. Cultivate your strength to land without a sound. Our quest in strength is to become better movers in smart bodies, not poor movers with a neurotic mindset.

For example...

Face backwards on the step mill to build a better booty, twist holding a plate to whittle down your waistline, wrap your midsection to lose belly fat, take this fat burner without fear of consequence, do not head to the gym without your pre-workout supplement, sweat in hot yoga to burn more fat... wait, is it April Fool's Day? Or, is your fitness overruled by your neuroticism?

Strength is using your mind to control the neuroticism and to search for knowledge. Be curious and cognizant. Activate your strength as you guide your decisions and allow patterns of behavior to either persist or desist.

Don't eat and exercise like it's your last day on this planet.

Your inner warrior knows you must eat like it's your first... because a battle of survival may await.

Word of the Week

Honestly, what would your day look like if you knew this was your last day on Earth? Probably not the 5am fitness class and a healthy breakfast, right? More likely, feet up at the pool with no sunscreen, a bottomless mimosa, planning out your woe-is-me pity party.

Strength is directing ourselves to eat and exercise like it's our first day... with the excitement and expectation to see the next... and the next. Strength is seeing past the neuroticism surrounding certain behaviors.

Speaking of neurotic... my husband is half-Sicilian, which is another way of saying he's never had a sunburn. He used to tan religiously... as a teenager to clear acne, in his twenties for photo shoots, and in his late thirties after he was diagnosed with cancer... skin cancer. He had lost the faith and was living like it was his last day on this planet. Now, he's not... because he has so much to explore, unlock, learn, and... love... love about me, but more critically, to love about himself.

But, the scale doesn't lie... or does it?

The only way you could burn more fat in a hot yoga class than on the treadmill is if you turned the temperature down. If you think hot yoga strips away body fat, you are overlooking the fact that our bodies have fantastic cooling systems. If you've ever taken hot anything, you know this. You sweat. You may even drop significant amounts of weight, but you will gain it all right back after you hydrate.

When I was skating professionally, some of us would sit in the sauna and most of us would consume nothing but a glass of wine on Friday nights… because we had weigh-ins on Saturday mornings. Yes, you can drop weight this way… temporary weight. But you are definitely not achieving transformation weight and you are definitely not doing something healthy. On the other hand, when temperatures are cold, our bodies have to "work" to stay warm. Hopefully, that encourages you to take up ice skating… or come to my new class, Freezing Yoga!

Lift more than you think you can.

Don't leave the gym with regret. And don't die with regret. Regret is a realization of under lifting or… under living. Ouch. We avoid it by challenging ourselves to experience life true to what our hearts have called us to do. We build strength so we can heal our fears. Healing our fears is our life mission.

"Curing is a physical experience. Healing is a spiritual one." ~Kris Carr

Don't buy, *invest*. Fly business… signal your worthiness.

My female frequent flyer friends often lament over how few women are sitting up in business class. All of us, but women especially, often choose the cheaper "seat"… particularly in areas of our career or self-investment that symbolize we are not worthy of luxury... or worthy of sitting with the big boys. The tragedy is we pinch off our dreams... and set back our daughters in the process.

But, everyone else is doing it... you mean, right now.

Do you know anyone still on the Atkins diet? That's how you should feel about diets or fads in general. Question their longevity... as they may undermine yours. If you say it is too expensive to eat healthily, I say it is too expensive to eat unhealthily... in terms of TCO... Total Cost of Ownership... ownership of you. Your long-term health costs. Your quality of life and movement. Personally, I never shop at Whole Foods because I can't stomach their prices. I don't buy supplements because I perceive them as a waste of money. I eat real food... from the grocery store... or even Domino's on occasion... because I know how to order it healthily. Food is not a reward, it's nourishment... for future strength opportunities.

Question the "news".

Sarah Ingmanson

When I was about to start my MBA at Wharton, my mother called me up frantically to tell me she had heard this "news" report that MBAs do not pay off. I exhaled and then agreed with her. Well, I agreed that many MBAs are probably not worth it. But I wasn't in that category. I had focus, intent, and strength... strength of desire, strength of purpose, strength of... a phenomenal business school. So, Wharton ended up being one of my finest life-enhancing investments... but I had to question the news, check in with myself, and... see next.

Stop worrying about what others think. It's zapping your strength.

If you're coming from a place of good intention and good heart, no else's opinion matters. (Not even your mother's... shhh!) You have something important to express... explore... unlock. Not more to accomplish, but more to learn... in order to get to know yourself better. To live an extraordinary life, you don't need extraordinary luck, money, or genetics, you just need extraordinary awareness. Awareness of yourself. This awareness opens your eyes to your innate strength.

Is it correlation or causation?

Just because you only see fit females facing backwards on the step mill, it doesn't mean this variation on the step mill builds a better booty. No, squats and lunges do. These women do tons of them... and probably have the habit of including protein in every meal. You could also say bright booty shorts build a better derrière... in that the only possible causation in either of these scenarios is the reverse—the better booty perhaps "caused" her to face backwards or to select her wardrobe... just to say, "Hey, look at me!"

What is the point of this exercise?

Is it to whittle down my waistline or to slip a disc? Twisting while holding a large plate is both the fastest way to add inches to your waistline and to slip a disc. My recommendation, stop doing this... well, unless you're a chiropractor who can profit from the perpetuation of this fallacy. A better exercise for your waistline with that heavy plate is to squat with it. Exercise mindfully... whether it's in the gym or out... look for patterns of behavior that are unintentionally harming you.

Forget the year... because your body has no clue.

If you were to start a fast or extreme diet, your body wouldn't take into consideration that it is 2015 AD and not 2015 BC. Its response would be the same... to stop and conserve everything. It doesn't realize that Starbucks is open or there is a ready supply of food in the refrigerator... that you're just not feeding it... because you are "committed". It thinks, there is no more food, so it must shut down and conserve energy. But, when we diet, we want to do the opposite. We want to rev up our metabolism so we can create that caloric deficit and lose weight inexpensively… in that, it doesn't require a lifelong membership at Weight Watchers or surgery… loose skin surgery.

THRIVE

Time to... THRIVE

Thrive to survive. To feel alive. To not compromise. To glow from the inside out.

"Survivors are attuned to the wonder of the world. The appreciation of beauty, the feeling of awe, opens the senses." ~Laurence Gonzales

Thriving happens when we don't force, control, or otherwise manage ourselves. We are drawn, magnetized, and mobilized to action instead... with a freedom to express ourselves authentically. This is where our true power resides... in the essence of who we are. Thriving is a feeling inside and it's most importantly an inner recognition that steps away from the self-deception that we somehow don't measure up.

Eckhart Tolle purports that 80-90% of our thinking is unnecessary and potentially harmful. When you "think" about it, this sounds pretty accurate. Thinking is beneficial when we are thriving... that is, when our thinking is inspired thought and geared toward creating and manifesting. However, most of our thinking is not inspired or geared in this direction. Instead, we are consumed with two places we will never return to or reach... the past and the future.

"If your mind isn't clouded by unnecessary things, you are in the best season of your life." ~Wu Men

Interestingly, the word, *thrive*, is most commonly used in reference to babies, flowers, industry, and... cancer cells.

These beings or entities know they measure up. They require optimal conditions and an optimal environment in which to grow... and they demand it... or are so compelling, we give it to them. Our mind works in much the same way, but the nourishment comes from our thoughts. Our thoughts create our mental environment. To deliver optimal nourishment to our minds, we have to train ourselves to think differently... and that means staying present... the only place that life actually happens.

"I do not fix problems. I fix my thinking. Then problems fix themselves."
~Louise Hay

We are the ones holding ourselves back from thriving... not the conditions we impose on our happiness, such as "when I get that job", "when my spouse does this", "after I retire"... blah, blah, blah. If we can't accept ourselves and our situations right where we are today, we will never thrive tomorrow... because tomorrow will never arrive. New conditions will replace old ones. To thrive, we have to journey deeper into ourselves... to a source of intelligence greater than thought. To access this place, we must feel centered and safe. In other words, we must be present.

Take some time this week to assess how much your thoughts are feeding places you will never be (past or future) or the place where you always are (present). If you are ready to get into the best season of your life, you need to practice feeding your presence more than your excess thinker... and this will empower you to THRIVE.

Word of the Week

THRIVE in an uncertain environment.

Put yourself in an environment where you don't know what will happen next. Unpredictable environments force us to be present. We're literally or figuratively at the edge of our seats. Where your warrior thrives.

THRIVE at the grocery store.

Select foods that assist in thriving. Food has an energy about it. To raise your energy, look at what is on your plate. Is there enough variety in texture, color, and type? Veggies and sprouted foods deliver a unique form of energy, detoxification, and aliveness into our being.

"When you're the conscious captain in your kitchen, you'll feel better mentally and physically." ~Kris Carr

Surround yourself with THRIVE-ing things. I have a personal preference for a certain baby, but flowers work nicely, too.

THRIVE by setting a healthy schedule.

Don't overdo it. Productive thought is creative thought, but understand that to be creative can involve feet up on the couch, walking along the beach, and enjoying good device-free dinner convo.

THRIVE in the mirror. No selfie necessary!

Repeat the following, "[Your name], I love you. I really, really do."

Sounds crazy, but highly effective in reversing that habit you have toward self-criticism and self-loathing. Mirror work helps to connect you with your inner child… the one who wants to be loved and has been suffering from years and years of neglect. If you've been told you are too trusting, you are gifted in seeing other people's inner child. To thrive yourself, though, you must become gifted in seeing and loving your own.

THRIVE in creativity with focused anything.

If meditation (focused breath) is not your thing, don't fret. How about focused doodling, cooking, gardening, dancing… focused anything you enjoy? Focused attention to something that soothes you is a meditative practice in staying present and will fuel your creativity and inner artist.

THRIVE mentally via focused teeth-brushing.

When we do daily tasks, such as brushing our teeth, our minds tend to wander away from what we're doing. By bringing ourselves back to the act of brushing our teeth, we are connecting to the present moment and heightening our awareness. Wisdom comes through more readily with heightened awarcness.

THRIVE in silence... i.e. turn off the damn phone!

"...the ability to be in constant contact, and our growing reliance on technology are all conspiring to create a noisy traffic jam between us and our place of insight and peace. Call it an iParadox: our smartphones are actually blocking our path to wisdom." ~Arianna Huffington

THRIVE with a mindful breath… and a built-in reminder to hydrate.

Pause throughout your workday for a mindful breath. While you're there, sip some water. Focus exclusively on both. Set reminders spaced 15-60 min apart to assist.

THRIVE with your next bite.

Chew. Bring your attention to it. The beauty of this is you enhance self-awareness and digestion in one activity… i.e. acceptable multi-tasking!

ACHIEVE

Take the "ache" out of ACHIEVE

"me, Me, ME!"

We are enticed to think achieving is something we do all by ourselves and through the toils of our effort and determination. However, in being enticed to this view of the word... world, we discount the collective resources available to us and cut ourselves off from a greater universal power.

To entice us further, a second definition of ACHIEVE has been added to reflect this mindset:

1. To perform or carry out with success; accomplish.
2. *To attain with effort or despite difficulty.*

Don't get me wrong. Effort and difficulty feel great... well, to your ego. Your ego wishes you to separate, work hard, and... suffer. But, suffering is optional. Achieve, as originally contemplated, means *to perform or carry out with success. To accomplish.* Success... accomplishment That is something you determine, define, and continue to refine.

Authors say it feels like channeling when inspiration flows into their writing. Athletes describe a sense of being "in the zone". In our finest moments—no matter what the pursuit, it feels like we're sourcing something greater than ourselves. From a place deeper than thought. That connective place of consciousness. To achieve, we need to access

Sarah Ingmanson

it. I mean, to really achieve the soul-satisfying, world-serving, heart-filling stuff that we are here to perform.

When the moment comes to step out on stage, onto the ice, up to the podium, or out on the playing field, we best be empty and open. An empty vessel is receptive. It's open to energy activated by our muscle memory… our physical, mental, and emotional muscle memory. It's a blend of knowing our script, and then forgetting about it. Experience comes into play here. Experience connects us to self-mastery. Slippage occurs when we allow experience to shut us down in fear, resentment, or the pursuit of the ego.

Go back and… remember who you are.

Encourage the desires. Activate the aliveness within you. Line up the dreams so the inspiration to act will come to you. So you attract other people, spaces, and places… the cooperative components to your dream. An alive dream… alive in the vibration of your energy… and activated from the passion in your heart.

"When I am there, in that golden circle where everything feels wonderful for no apparent reason, I try to memorize the feeling, the terrain, the scenery. I have noticed how full I feel at those moments, with an overwhelming sense of lightness about all things. I know that this is our natural state and that the purpose of our lives is to achieve it consistently." ~Marianne Williamson

Should you wish to take the "ache" out of ACHIEVE, you are left with: "I've"… as in "I have"… What do *you* have? What do you *want to* have?

Eat to ACHIEVE.

Whether it's a physical or mental endeavor, both body and mind require fuel for creative energy. It's a requirement, not a nice-to-have. The body and brain require nutrients to synthesize thought and execute tasks. Your body is giving you plenty of signals. It's your choice whether to listen.

Lose the guilt to ACHIEVE.

We are our own worst enemies. That's why meditation and self-awareness practices are so important. Not only do they help us relax, focus, and feel more peaceful inside, we notice the inner critic right away... and become expert on silencing him or her.

Suit up to ACHIEVE.

Put on your power pumps. From head to toe, dress the part. Leave no detail behind. You are your personal business card.

Stay to ACHIEVE.

Stay in the pose... the set... the exercise (jogging, writing, crunching numbers included) with dedication and deliberate intent. Feel the difference this shift from obligation to dedication makes.

Show up to ACHIEVE.

Show up every day. Not just when you feel like it. The best stuff comes through us when we are feeling the full spectrum of emotions... when we are playing our role as human. Make it an important part of your life if it's an important part of your heart.

Delegate to ACHIEVE.

Word of the Week

Trust others. Trust activates the collaborative resources and releases the pressure… the pressure you put on yourself to be indispensable and to "get it all done". You only seek this kind of external validation when you feel empty and unworthy inside. You let go of it as soon as you realize people love you for who you are, not how much you can do.

"It's not about being indispensable at work, it's about being irreplaceable as a human." ~Nancy Levin

Align the clock to ACHIEVE.

Figure out your optimal creative time and sync accordingly. I prefer to write or read first thing in the morning because that's when my mind is clearest and most alert, but mornings are not typically my quiet time anymore. So I've adjusted my creative clock to sync with my daughter's naps… to use my weekends more productively… and to sneak in some time while my husband is making dinner. I notice waves of creativity right after I teach, exercise, or indulge in a facial or massage, so I'll stop for a few minutes to journal then, too.

Don't be shy to ACHIEVE.

I'm a self-proclaimed introvert. My natural tendency is to shy away from networking and schmoozing. There are times in life, though, that call for us to network, schmooze, and… speak up. Yes, send that email. Ask. You never know which connection is going to be the one… the one today or maybe the one tomorrow… or maybe the one 10 years from now. The one that will open up doors for you. Being shy is not cute. Being shy is playing scared. And, it's holding you back from all the good stuff life wishes to serve you.

Follow your inner guidance to ACHIEVE.

What feels right to you? Go from there. You can't achieve in the shadows of others or under their limited viewpoints. You must follow your own calling to truly achieve what feels right in your heart and head.

"A Warrior does not spend his days trying to play the role that others have chosen for him." ~Paulo Coelho

Create distance to ACHIEVE.

Distance... physical, mental, emotional. When we are so tuned in to everything going on in the world, in other people's lives, we lose our personal edge. We need to tune out to tune in. Consider how you can tune out the mindless chatter and assaults to the psyche that are shifting your focus away from the stuff that really matters... to you... and what you wish to achieve.

ENGAGE

Let the fat lady sing… ENGAGE

A hand shake, a diamond ring, a signature, a tightening of the abdominal muscles, an intense pose or just an intense eye gaze… there are various ways to ENGAGE. But, to stay engaged, you must commit to one thing.

"Be ridiculously in charge of your attention… because what you look for will be enlivened in your awareness." ~Sarah McLean

Sounds easy enough. We should be able to control what we pay attention to… right? The complexity arises when we ENGAGE over long distances. Especially, a certain, exceptionally long distance…

"The longest journey a man must take is the eighteen inches from his head to his heart." ~Unknown

In taking this journey, we connect one level deeper to the essence of who we are and why we are here. Soul-level questions. How-to-live-lifefully questions. What does that look like for you? How do you know you're on the right path? Easy… ish. You ENGAGE. You truly engage.

Word of the Week

ENGAGE long enough to return to the essence of who you are. Our human conditioning is corrupt, not our soul…

Conditioning goes like this: Every action produces a memory… a memory of experience. This memory then triggers a desire… a desire to repeat or a desire to reject… also known as the yum or yuck response. Of course, we may misinterpret. We may think it was the doughnut that made us feel better. But, as long as we pay attention, we gain awareness and neutrality. Self-awareness to see what we are doing and the separation to assess why we are doing it. From that place of neutral self-awareness, we can choose to repeat the behavior or, we can stop and choose a different behavior that feels more nurturing and nourishing to our inner warrior.

ENGAGE your inner fat girl. Listen to what she needs to say.

Sarah Ingmanson

"I still think like a fat girl… it's letting go of the negativity and even though that is a good thing, it's still like letting go of an old friend." ~*Anonymous*

We all have a fat girl persona. Send her love, light, and respect. Give her air time because she's not going to die if you don't… actually, she's going to act out like an angry toddler if you don't.

I detest laziness. I would be momentarily furious if you called me lazy. As a result, I have a tendency to spread myself too thin and become borderline neurotic about my productivity. It does not mean, however, that I am not lazy. It means I'm denying Lazy Lana… the lazy girl within.

When we associate so personally with the undesired behavior, we can't separate and stay neutral. This triggers unkind feelings of shame, embarrassment, and guilt. We become the behavior rather than merely the experience of behavior.

ENGAGE your excellence, not your perfectionist.

Controlling yourself to be perfect or ideal in some superhuman sense is NOT the way to engage your excellence. Unless you're looking for meltdown, breakdown, or any other kind of letdown, do not proceed with the self-denial promised in perfectionism. We are all things… including the things that irritate us the most in other people (our divine mirrors)!

Word of the Week

ENGAGE with compassion and acceptance.

When we realize we all have the full spectrum of emotions and personality traits, it becomes easier to accept others and, more importantly, to self-accept. It's not that we desire to be fat or lazy, it's that these personas have a message for us. They are delivering a desire or need that we are not fulfilling for ourselves.

Don't get motivated, ENGAGE.

Motivation doesn't work because motivation keeps you up in your mind, in that place of what you *should* do. Should-ing yourself is not being kind to yourself… it's leading you down the path of self-sabotage, self-hatred, and into a place of unworthiness.

That's why we have Motivation Monday, New Year's Resolutions, and a gazillion dollar weight loss industry. Motivation does not get to the heart of the matter. We are not taking that all-important journey from head to heart. When we engage, we are. We are connecting the two. Closing the gap. The gap within ourselves. Alleviating that dull pervasive ache associated with not living the life you were meant to.

ENGAGE with a promise, a pledge… or a trip to the pawn shop!

The word, *engage,* originally meant 'to pawn or pledge something'. By the 16th and 17th centuries, the definition embodied doing something, such as signing a contract, involving oneself in an activity, or entering into combat. A promise of sorts. A promise to the fat girl to take the next best step in life. A promise to your fiancé that you are one step away from the altar.

Word of the Week

ENGAGE with a smoke signal.

Take a stance, sign up for the race, strike up a conversation, or in any other way, put yourself out there. In doing so, you send a smoke signal up to the Universe that you are ready for the next set of instructions... and to yourself that you are one step away from the ultimate goal... your expanded happiness.

PASSION

Less wine, more sushi, please… PASSION

A fruit… a fire within… not something you follow… it's something that drags you. Passion gives you purpose and courage.

"Passion makes you shave your head and move to Tibet." ~Elizabeth Gilbert

OK, that's one possibility! More pertinently, if you don't have it at this exact moment, relax. Let it find you. Don't punish yourself or attempt to locate it frantically. Understand that passion is designed to ebb and flow in our lives. Passion can be misused as a synonym for perfection just to make us feel badly about where we are currently in the ebb and flow. So, when passion has seemingly abandoned you, start more gently with curiosity and work up from there.

"Every creative process is a break in logic… otherwise it's an algorithm." ~Deepak Chopra

Passion is a type of attraction. Often, we can't quite put our finger on why we feel so devoted to it. Passion seems to have its own prana or life force within it that entices and coaxes us to step out of fear and into life.

"Passion is the genesis of genius." ~Galileo Galileo

Word of the Week

Passion is the beginning. The thing that inspires our dedication and commitment. Passion elicits our talents and expands our preconceived notion of what is possible. It arrives in our life with a personal message:

Stretch assignment enclosed. Are you ready? Well, are you?!

You see, passion can be a bit impatient. It is more like sushi than red wine… it should be consumed as soon as it appears. It resembles a start-up in temperament. We observe the characteristics of passion in the fruit bearing its name.

The passion fruit is a vigorous, climbing vine that clings by tendrils to almost any support. It can grow quickly once established, but it must have strong support. It is generally short-lived.

Passion fruit is indigenous to Brazil and other countries in South America. (What a surprise…) And, like our human passions, these plant passions require fertile soil. Otherwise, our attention goes to survival, not to thrive-al.

So, our objective this week is to become a vessel for passion. We work toward clearing ourselves of passion-killing neural grooves. Neural grooves are formed in repetition. The ones we need to clear are the stories we keep telling ourselves that keep us stuck and stagnant. Rather than protecting us, they in fact paralyze us into living small and scared.

Sleep to restore harmony, heal, and rest/reset the mind. The body and mind repair themselves in sleep.

Stress of any sort puts us into fight or flight mode. Perpetual fight or flight mode invites dis-ease and weakens our constitution. In stress, we focus on survival, whether the threat is real or (mis)perceived.

Move at least once an hour. Movement of any sort. Just move. Bonus points for dancing the tango…

Externally-motivated goals cannot sustain passion. Being of service can. Being externally-motivated entails acting out someone else's agenda for appearances or out of fear of scarcity, being unlovable or, in any other way, not enough. In contrast, being of service reflects generosity of spirit and passion for the activity of engagement.

Insecurity and fear lure us to shut down and turn away from our passion. No matter how much passion surrounds you, you cannot feel the embrace unless you unfold your arms to receive it.

Hydration. Water. Water. Water. Restore your body's balance. Dehydration disrupts digestion and impedes physical performance and blood flow. Water is your best form of defense against headaches and muscular tension. It's hard to be expressive when consumed by pain or tension.

Starving artist no more! Eat for passion. Beyond passion fruit, there are foods thought to be natural aphrodisiacs… foods that affect our hormones, brain chemistry, energy and stress levels. Foods, such as basil, asparagus, almonds, avocado, garlic, and oysters.

Excessive thinking or increased levels of mental activity block our intuition. Intuition is the bridge to our creativity. Noise and distraction add to the mental activity, loosening our concentration and needlessly busying our minds. Without creativity, we are no different from robots. Passion feeds us creatively in a way that thinking cannot.

Meditate to lower your mental activity and truly connect at a higher level. Set a timer for 30 minutes. Yes, 3-0! Sit through any discomfort associated with stillness. For optimal results, do this twice a day; once upon awakening and once right before dinner.

SURPRISE

It's a... SURPRISE!

SURPRISE! You've got... mail, the job offer, cancer

SURPRISE! You are... pregnant, lost, fired

SURPRISE! It's... a boy, a girl, twins?!

SURPRISE! Your flight has been... delayed, cancelled, rerouted

SURPRISE! There is a... party, call, letter for you

SURPRISE! It's an... announcement, emergency, earthquake

SURPRISE! We have a... verdict, diagnosis, outcome you were not expecting...

Key words, *not expecting*. Whatever "it" is in the context of SURPRISE, you were not expecting it. Surprise! Welcome to life... where things are often closer than they appear... or, they don't appear at all. We learn again and again to soften our expectations and trust our outcomes to be perfect for, maybe not what we want, but what we need. The gift may not be obvious at first glance. It often is not. Otherwise, we wouldn't have been surprised.

"Sometimes, in the middle of battles not of his choosing, he is taken by surprise, but there is no point in running away. Those battles will merely follow him."
Paulo Coelho

Even modern-day battles, such as flight delays...

SURPRISE reminds us... hey, you're alive, you survived that painful awful thing... or maybe you're going through it right now. But, lo and behold, there's something... many things... so many things to be grateful for in this moment. Shift your awareness and acknowledge something in gratitude right now. Gratitude breaks the downward spiral of anxiety and negativity.

SURPRISE is an opportunity to self-soothe when we notice it elicits our fight-or-flight response, a.k.a. stress.

What helps you counteract stress? Is it yoga and meditation, or dancing and good go-to sessions with a close friend? Decompress in whichever ways make sense and work for you... and you have access to in your particular "battlefield".

Word of the Week

SURPRISE reminds us to lighten up.

The world isn't out to *get* you, it is out to *teach* you. Soften your rigid expectations of how things should work out... and just let them work out.

Add love to the SURPRISE.

Clap when you fall... as my daughter did in learning to walk. Perfect the art of soft landings with a lighter feeling in your heart. In a baby, it involves bending one's knees... and clapping. FYI : clapping helps with everything!

Sarah Ingmanson

SURPRISE may tempt us to shy away from life, to withdraw from pain, and to recluse into a more limited sense of self and the frontier of possibilities.

This isn't the answer or the gift, though... So, what is? Go one level deeper and see if you can find the answer(s).

"No one person can anticipate all of life. In fact, overpreparation is yet another way to wall ourselves in from life. Rather, we can only prepare for how we might respond to the gift of surprise that often moves in on us faster than our reflex to resist." ~Mark Nepo

SURPRISE may change your voice... or leave you speechless.

How you respond to any surprises says a lot about you. How do you treat the person serving you when there is an element of surprise... for example, a flight delay? How can you continue to communicate your essence even when surprise happens? For it will... life guarantees it.

Word of the Week

SURPRISE is a brief mental and physiological state... a startle response experienced as the result of an unexpected event. Detected in the face with raised eyebrows, eyes opening wide, a dropped jaw, and experienced in the heart with the heart rate quickening and emotions rising.

Notice your surprise response, how it impacts your body, vision, and flow. See if you can detect it in another's eyes, facial expression, or behavior. Use your wisdom of experience and your long-term vision to guide your response and perspective.

SURPRISE calls out ignorance because, in surprise, we reveal a gap... a gap between our assumptions and our expectations, and a gap between our expectations and our reality.

We assume worldly event A means outcome B, but then we witness outcome C. In the acknowledgement of our ignorance, we learn our predictive models may need some fine-tuning. This allows us to avoid or anticipate the next crash... and practice soft landings.

"...any moment of interest or pain or adversity can surprise us into the larger totality of life, breaking our current limits and allowing us the chance to redefine ourselves in regard to the larger sense that is upon us." ~Mark Nepo

REACH

Out through your fingertips... REACH

REACH with your arm... your heart... your intention... your voice.

REACH for a dream... a goal... a desire.

REACH to serve... to touch... to expand... to ignite.

REACH in spirit... in service... in gratitude.

REACH out for length... for depth... for more.

REACH for your life.

Reach is a measurement of arm span for boxers and MMA fighters. A longer reach becomes an advantage in a fight... and in your life. Out of the ring, it matters less whether your "wing" span is long, it matters more that you believe your arms are wings. With wings, you feel worthiness to reach. To keep reaching. And then, to reach for more...

Reach relates to your sense of self-worth because you won't reach when you feel undeserving of ease, abundance, honesty, happiness, healing...(fill in your blank here). And, how you reach is just as important as whether you reach. Both come back to your underlying commitments.

Word of the Week

"We have to unconceal all the beliefs that keep us from attaining our dreams. I call these underlying commitments because they are agreements we have made with ourselves to not reach our true goals. Whether you decide to go after your dreams or not, it's important to question what's driving you, as well as what gets in the way of your heart's desires." ~Deborah Ford

Where is the conflict? Which underlying commitments are sabotaging your reach? How are your beliefs about your talent, intelligence, genetics, luck, or past experience factoring into your considerations of how or whether to reach. Reach for that thing you want. What if it was right at the end of your fingertips? How would that change your approach today... this week... this life?

"Step out of your comfort zone and be that person that sometime hides inside. Who knows what will emerge... when you REACH for what you deserve. ~Stacey Lei Krauss

Reaching has a certain boldness about it. Especially when like-minded individuals assemble. In the "reaching for", you attract conspiring components. The intention with which you reach directly corresponds to what you retrieve, though.

REACH with flexible strength.

Flexibility in mind and body. A flexible mindset is not a doormat; it is open to new ideas and accepting of differing viewpoints. A flexible body is our armor against injury. Both are the alleviating agents of tension.

"Tension is who you think you should be. Relaxation is who you are." ~Chinese Proverb

REACH in a different direction with one small change.

This one small change must be a challenge to strengthen your "reach" muscle and to empower you from a "fix" mentality to a forward "evolving" motion. Eliminate one destructive or nonessential thing you find yourself reaching for…

"Pick something that feels at least a little bit edgy… where are you on autopilot in a way that does not serve you?"~Nancy Levin

REACH with sacrifice… selectively. Sacrifice involves putting another or something else first. Sacrifice can be noble when directed toward a dream, desire, calling or cause that makes your heart sing. But when sacrifice entails giving up these things to make someone else happy, less threatened, or temporarily satisfied, there is no nobility, there is pleasing. In pleasing others, we lose. Loss of self. Loss of time and energy.

"If I spend my life pleasing people, I spend my life." ~Cheryl Richardson

Word of the Week

REACH for enhanced expression... a bigger calorie burn... an opening of the chakras... a release of feel-good endorphins.

As a fitness instructor, my least favorite question to receive is, "How many calories will this class burn?" The answer always lies in your reach. The reach of your leg in hip-hinge, the reach for weights as you load up your squat bar, the reach of your arm as you side-plank... the reach for muscle-preserving protein in your meals.

REACH with worthy goals.

Your goals. Not someone else's. Not what society, a friend, or a family member suggests. What *you* want while understanding that any outward changes are preceded with an internal transformation. Transformed thinking leads to transformed being.

In meditation, ask yourself, "What do you want?". It is one of the soul-level questions designed to bring us back to our true essence with enlightened ideas and inspiration. Try it. You might be surprised by your answers.

REACH with assistance.

When you can't reach for something by yourself, please ask for help. Going it alone doesn't make you more lovable. Being who you are does.

REACH with linguistic cognizance.

Be aware of what you say. Omit the word, "just", and any words describing shortage or an undesired state in your reach statements.

For example, saying, "I just want a job that pays the bills", will ensure you JUST get that… with a bit of struggle and a bunch of drudgery… but certainly nothing more. "I'm becoming so accident-prone… and fat in my old age," reaps, "More accidents and sticky pounds, please."

REACH, don't preach.

Word of the Week

We can waste a lot of energy, time, and resources explaining, defending, convincing, or otherwise justifying our positions. Question the necessity of these conversations and how they are impacting your energy reserves to reach with pure intention. An impure intention is one involving anger or animosity. "I'll show them!" is less potent than working toward a vision with positive inspiration and personal integrity. When energy is dispersed into fueling negativity, you become distracted and exposed to so-called energy vampires.

REACH for a better feeling thought.

Thoughts create momentum and tend to spiral (downward) quickly. From a place of awareness, task yourself to reach for a thought that feels a little better… a little lighter. Build from there with authenticity, not denial. For example, it's too great a reach to go from, "This sucks" to "This is awesome", but maybe you can soften it a bit. Find one blessing or ounce of gratitude in the situation. Realize the only thing we have control over are our thoughts. In other words, self-soothing is always an option.

REACH for quality.

Stop filling your places or spaces with junk. Reach for quality when picking out your next book, meal, company. Call 1-800-Got-Junk, clean out your fridge or perhaps your social calendar.

FREEDOM

A worthwhile goal... FREEDOM

What do you need freedom from? Is it something tangible, such as a person, place, or thing? Or is it possibly an emotion that is holding you captive? Close your eyes and let one word come to your mind. Imagine life without it. Contemplate habits, beliefs, and thought patterns. What no longer serves you at this age or stage? Trade it out... see this word as a symbol of your bondage... and nothing less than your freedom is on the line.

We struggle when we feel tied down by our situations, our resources, our abilities... or even our looks. But in this place of disappointment, resentment, self-disgust, or despair, we contribute to the downward spiral. We shrink. We fester. We fatigue.

"Are you going to live 90 years? Or, live the same year 90 times? ~Wayne Dyer

You don't fit into a box? The good news is you weren't supposed to. The bad news is most people don't realize this. So, see stereotyping for what it is—a tool of ignorance and judgement... and what it is not—within the arsenal of love and acceptance. Stereotyping will probably not kill you, but it has the potential to zap you... if you step into the role of victim or martyr.

FREEDOM is not achieved through unnecessary sacrifice.

Sacrifice is the unfortunate side effect of playing victim or martyr. When we sacrifice in these ways, we remove our choice and therefore our personal power and eventually what feels like our freedom. If we allow sacrifice to persist within the body, we create resentment and dis-ease.

FREEDOM can also relate to your decision to dress a certain way… or to break out of a life that someone else has set for you.

Word of the Week

FREEDOM is a worthwhile goal.

FREEDOM allows you to speak your truth.

Freedom is felt primarily in the throat as our ability to self-express. This can affect your voice and the way you refrain from speaking your truth.

Sarah Ingmanson

FREEDOM resonates within.

When you think about your personal values and goals, ask yourself, "are these mine or someone else's?" Because, true happiness is in congruence with yours. Those values and goals that resonate within you.

"Too frequently, we think we're choosing peace and comfort over freedom. But, in truth, we're sacrificing our inner peace in hopes of outer peace." ~Nancy Levin

Word of the Week

FREEDOM is being who you are.

Maybe it's being allowed to get married or maybe it's allowing yourself to be loved. Either way, you are unrestrained... uncensored... and unflippingly authentic.

RESPECT

Secure your oxygen mask first... RESPECT

Respect. We think we have to demand it, command it, and continuously earn it, but real respect (read: self-respect) requires nothing of the sort. We give our power away when we rely on others... for their judgement, their validation, their permission. Respect must come from a place of wholeness for it to be deeply-rooted. Once rooted, we simply breathe into it and watch it expand.

"Secure your oxygen mask first."

In the event of an emergency, the only way you'd secure your oxygen mask first is if you believed it was both necessary and important. When you feel disrespected, there's a good chance you are not securing your own mask first...

Like many things, respect is an inside job. How deeply rooted is your self-respect? As you breathe into your own oxygen mask, notice how you feel more oxygen available to breathe into other places, spaces, and souls.

Word of the Week

RESPECT the unfolding.

Where you are is perfect. Find contentment in Tree pose. Exhale. Detach. Believe in abundance. Practice balance. Use your arms to get rid of what you don't need, gather what you do, and let it manifest.

RESPECT your body.

Flexibility is needed to perform exercise well… intensely… and healthily. It is also needed just to move through life well and to feel good inside our bodies. Out of the three strengths—muscular, endurance, and flexibility, flexible strength is the only one we lose without daily maintenance. And, as we build the other types of strength, we often contribute to the loss of flexibility through muscular tension and endurance posture (e.g. cycling). So, caring for your body is an essential way to breathe respect back into self. Triangle with rotation layers in torso rotation. Rotation to detoxify from the inside out. Triangle to symbolize the three points of ourselves: mind, body, spirit.

RESPECT fuels self-confidence.

Hinge forward from your hip on one leg with confidence. Strong, centered, and balanced. Arms out to the side for balance or reaching forward for more. Lift your leg higher as your confidence increases.

RESPECT breeds happiness.

Lift your head all the way up with your chest open and hands clasped at heart. Release adrenaline. Let this heart opener counteract the cell phone hunch. The *anahata* (heart) chakra translates from Sanskrit as "unstruck". Unstruck meaning your heart before it was hurt by anything or anybody.

RESPECT invites forgiveness.

Forgive yourself. Forgive others. Sweep to release your spine. Reach way back and release the past. With a strong exhale, swing your arms by your side with a deep knee bend, getting rid of stale energy, negative thought patterns, and resentment.

RESPECT the silent and burning desire that's within you—don't scoff at it…

"When you trust in your inner vision, you're trusting the same wisdom that created you." ~Wayne Dyer

Sarah Ingmanson

RESPECT into reverence.

When you feel respectful, a reverence follows. It is not forced or obligatory. It's heartfelt and sincere. Reverence for beauty, sacrifice, purity, quality, thoughtfulness. Deference for expertise, knowledge, and experience. We become curious, interested, observant, and we embrace learning (again). We see value all around us and, in that awareness, we heighten the value of everything around us—our interactions, our connections, and our experiences.

BELIEVE

BELIEVE... in what you wish to see

When you believe, you trigger a chain reaction of events... in your body and in your mind. You let go of the what-if's and you open yourself up to new possibilities.

"I used to be a dancer. When I lose all this weight, I'll be 'her' again."
~Anonymous

Why not be her right now? Because you won't *see* her, until you *believe* in her.

When you don't believe, you stay on the sidelines... of your life. You operate within self-imposed limitations. You stay in fear. You lose curiosity. And, most tragically, you close down. But often, life happens to give you another chance. Another chance to believe. To believe you can write a new chapter... or to believe you can't and so you relive an old one. The choice is up to you. Belief simply powers up your expectation.

What do you believe? You need look no further than your life to answer this question. Our beliefs limit us and, interestingly, most of our beliefs come from other people. Our subconscious, in particular, is programmed with strong beliefs from our childhood. These are the most difficult to rewrite because they were ingrained at an early age... and perhaps passed down over generations, so we are not even aware of their changeable existence and overriding impact. Consider these common ones:

You must work hard. Life is tough. Winning is everything. The world is a cruel place. Women only care about money. Men can't be trusted. You'll get fat (and infertile) over forty.

Enough. The problem is...

"We tend to experience in life what we identify with in our beliefs." ~Gregg Braden

Imagine if your beliefs empowered you into greater living? Fewer limitations, less distrust... more confidence, conviction, and competence. The fantastic news is they can. With awareness and intention, we can reprogram them.

If you are embarking on a big life change or a long journey of commitment, belief is incredibly important. It is everything. Because your body hears absolutely everything you say... and worse (perhaps), everything you think. So, whether you're contending with Stage 3 cancer or triple-digit weight loss... leaving an abusive relationship or moving to a new city, wherever you find yourself making scary change, you are likely face-to-face with a deeply hidden belief that has held you back in the past.

The key to freedom lies within ourselves... as a belief (or set of beliefs) we need to realign with our current dreams and sources of happiness.

More good news:

"Our subconscious mind cannot tell the difference between reality and an imagined thought or image." ~Robert Collier

Word of the Week

BELIEVE in refinement.

Learning to engage a specific muscle leads to superior form, muscular balance, and smarter training. Proprioception is a fancy word for your body in space. Where your fist is relative to your shoulder as you begin to rotate. More refined movement leads to a more refined physique and a smarter body.

"Believe that you can twist deeper... believe that you can find yourself again."
~willPower & grace

BELIEVE in the power of touch.

A soft hand on the shoulder brings relief to a grieving heart and delivers a caring message. After a baby is born, skin-to-skin contact assures the scared little one of safety within the familiar warmth of the maternal embrace. How can you use touch to expand your embrace and presence in the world?

BELIEVE in your worthiness.

You deserve to be on stage, to sit at the table, to have the wealth and abundance you seek. As you believe in your worthiness, the world believes in you.

BELIEVE in small acts of kindness.

Treating the person in line behind you to a free cup of coffee brings a smile of appreciation and sets off a ripple effect of kindness in our world. Believe in compassion. It's a world-changer.

Word of the Week

Show that you BELIEVE it.

Communicate your belief through your body language. How is your posture? Engage the postural muscles front and back. What does the speed or manner of your walk reveal about your belief in yourself? Over 50% of our communication comes through how we "speak" with our bodies. As you find your eyes in the mirror or make eye contact with another, ask yourself, "What am I communicating?" Confident belief or... something else?

BELIEVE in your vision. Imagine a new reality. Keep it strongly in your mind. Often change requires a long-term commitment and therefore a steadfast vision. To stay on course, however, requires tremendous belief. Belief in what's best for you.

Sarah Ingmanson

BELIEVE in your spiritual perfection and innate worthiness all along the way.

Wear blinders to any media or social pressures that are not serving your best future interest.

"We live our lives based on what we believe about our world, ourselves, our capabilities, and our limits." ~Gregg Braden

COMMITMENT

Glue your dreams and desires... COMMITMENT

Commitment is a promise to another, a cause, and, ultimately, to yourself. To stay true to yourself. To stay calmly seated even when unexpected turbulence arises and your heart begins to race. Commitment, in its highest form, is a promise to never abandon yourself.

Commitment is a vehicle of love. A symbolic honoring of your purest intentions. A contract to keep yourself accountable to your dreams and desires, to what you love, to what makes your heart sing.

Commitment is a set of binoculars that can see past the storm... and past the separation or the lack you fear. You need not be "right" to feel safe in a relationship, you just need commitment at a heart-to-heart level.

Beware, though, of compromise sneaking into your commitments. Compromise is fear-based (e.g. if I don't give in, x will happen) while commitment elicits deeper love. When compromise isn't there, all parties involved have to figure out the highest and best way to proceed. You are not caving in. Not this time. Your presence is needed. And you cultivate a practice of presence with another. A precedent of strength and, ultimately, a call to your magnificence.

"There is great fear. From those who seek compromise." ~Joshua G. Johnson

Sarah Ingmanson

Commitment is planting a seed, nurturing that seed, and providing the optimal conditions for this seed to grow… and flourish. This seed can be represented in your garden, your children, your relationships, your career, and your fitness. In all of the above, your commitments require nurturing and attention.

"We can complain because rose bushes have thorns, or rejoice because thorn bushes have roses." ~Abraham Lincoln

Commitment begins sentences with "I am", not "I will". We seek to attract and energize our best, not to keep things an arm's length away and always out of reach.

"There was a long time when I was the only person in the world who called myself a writer… You have to be the first one to say it." ~Elizabeth Gilbert

Commitment requires dedicated effort. If you are committed to being a writer, you write every day. If you are an athlete, you commit to training every day. If you are injured, you commit to your body's healing and the self-regulation that entails.

Commitment is the glue of your dreams and desires. It holds things together even on the days when things appear to be falling apart. Commitment challenges the negative committee convening in your head and holds your higher vision… at least, it does when the commitment is worthwhile.

When are our commitments not worthwhile? Glad you asked!

Word of the Week

Restructure the enslaving COMMITMENTS.

Do your commitments empower or enslave you? Notice whether you feel heavy or light when you think about your various commitments. Can you offload or restructure any of the "heavy" ones?

Locate the emergency exit in your COMMITMENTS.

Do your commitments have an expiration date or an exit strategy? For example, have you ever committed to weight loss for an event... did it stay off after the event? If not, why? How can you revise and improve the commitment this time? How can it serve you in the long-run?

Renege your COMMITMENTS to the *wrong* numbers.

Age. Weight. Salary. IQ. Think about how various numbers define, limit, or constrain you from living the life you were born to live.

Keep yourself healthy *in spite of* your COMMITMENTS.

Are your commitments energy-depleting or energy-giving? Sometimes, our commitments choose us… or we choose them despite the depletion. If they are energetically depleting, are you taking care of yourself sufficiently through other outlets? And, are these outlets healthy?

Renew your keeper COMMITMENTS.

Word of the Week

Breathe life into your keeper commitments with a caress, a change of scenery, a new perfume, or maybe just a pause to acknowledge your heartfelt gratitude... in heart-to-heart (H2H) plank.

In H2H plank, we create a symbolic heart with our hands and align it with our true heart. The heart chakra is a bridge between the lower and upper chakras integrating the physically manifest with the spiritual. In essence, connecting the body to the mind. When we feel disconnected from our bodies, we need to look at our commitments. What are we committed to that our hearts are rejecting at some level?

Express your COMMITMENTS.

Is there congruence between your stated commitments and your day-to-day expressions? Bring awareness to your words, actions, feelings. How are they aligned or in opposition to your commitments?

Define COMMITMENT for yourself.

What do you see when you close your eyes and say the word, *commitment*? Is it surprising? Journal about it.

Connect your COMMITMENTS back to your overarching purpose.

Are your commitments pleasing to your soul? In meditation, ask yourself, "What do I want?", "What is my purpose?", and "What am I grateful for?" See how they relate and connect you to your worthwhile commitments.

POWER

It's in the landing... POWER

Power is a force within ourselves. A force of our unique talents to create. A force of our focused thoughts to manifest. A force of our open willingness to see our lives with new eyes. Force requires an energy source. Our power is fueled by confidence, connectedness, and living out our truth. When desire gains momentum and takes flight, we enter new patterns of orbit. Watch out world. Here we *are*.

Power is the rate of doing work or the rate of using energy. They are equivalent, aren't they? As you think of your productivity at work or your calorie burn in the gym, contemplate your power in both respects—the rate at which you are working and the rate at which you are consuming energy.

Power allows us to move quickly and forcefully when we need to. But it also allows us to pull back and wait for the right opportunity to strike. As demonstrated in the exercise of the week—the power knee—power requires complete control over the movement. Being able to perform a movement at variable speed takes skill and control, and this ability manifests greater power.

So, we practice... landing. Quarterbacks learn how to get hit by defensive players. A figure skater practicing a new jump, a diver mastering a new dive, or a baby learning how to walk, these "athletes" learn how to fall to avoid (or mitigate) injury. An instructor watches her class and learns which cues are "landing" well. There is experience and there is feedback. We don't usually land perfectly the first time out, but our power increases as we learn to land softly. We learn to embrace the landing even when it's not the landing we are seeking or striving for.

Practice your POWER up as well as down. Become powerfully effective in your movement. Practice landings that are soft and precise.

Picture the following scenarios and ask yourself which role would feel more POWERful in the moment, after the moment, and watching the moment (e.g. in televised replay):

You are the subordinate. How does your power grow or diminish when forced to do something vs. choosing to do something?

Word of the Week

Picture the following scenario and ask yourself which role would feel more POWERful in the moment, after the moment, and watching the moment (e.g. in televised replay):

You are a person of "authority" (e.g., manager, boss, teacher, parent). Scenario 1, you make another person do something. Scenario 2, you inspire the other person to do something.

Notice any POWER struggles in your work, personal relationships, or casual interactions (e.g. at the grocery store).

Is gratitude absent? Is misunderstanding or miscommunication rampant? Does one party hold a sense of superiority or righteousness? Can you detect fear in the struggle?

Picture the following scenario and ask yourself which role would feel more POWERful in the moment, after the moment, and watching the moment (e.g. in televised replay):

An argument in which one person is yelling at another. The other person stands calmly without saying a word.

Reflect on a POWERful time in your life.

Did you feel powerful at the time? How did your feelings toward the situation change over time? Explore why.

Word of the Week

Cultivate a POWERful presence through your words, voice, eye contact, and example.

Our goal is to see ourselves accurately… to realize that we are, in fact, powerful beyond measure.

"Our deepest fear is that we are powerful beyond measure. We ask ourselves, who am I to be brilliant, gorgeous, talented and fabulous? Actually, who are you not to be? Your playing small does not serve the world. And as we let our own light shine, we unconsciously give other people permission to do the same."
~Marianne Williamson

VISION

Turn your eyes skyward... VISION

Our vision is more than the image taken in by our eyes. It is the way in which we see the world. The unique twist we put on what we see. Our feelings reveal how we see things and our behavior typically follows. When our behavior diverges from that feeling place, we start to experience a disconnect inside. This is where holding a vision can be willPower-ful. A vision serves to realign us back to our purpose and where we intend to be.

Our vision expands beyond the present moment as we interpret the past and contemplate the future. Vision assimilates what we know with what we wish to experience.

Sometimes, our vision is blurry. Other times, it is crystal clear. We need both to grow in our willPower. When we focus too heavily on the fuzzy parts (typically in the "how"), we disallow the best possible outcome. We need to envision what we want and then let go of the "how the heck" to attract the conspiring elements.

Your vision carries the potential for power or paralysis. It all depends on you and the twist you put on what you see. Vision contains power when it transforms a situation beyond your wildest expectations into an even higher vision. Or, it paralyzes you to cling onto a solitary outcome that you weren't meant to live.

Vision is the mechanism through which we dare to make the first bold step and then carry through with the necessary next steps.

Detach from the blurry parts you aren't meant to see, so you can be receptive to your life in its highest form.

Triangle symbolizes the trinity of mind, body, spirit. Aligning yourself in triangle pose allows you to turn your head upward to your vision and away from the fear, distractions, and limitations that may be clouding your vision.

Keep your VISION on the destination.

Know where you're heading. Check in with your internal compass to make sure you haven't floated adrift.

"Without a destination in mind, there is no journey; we just wander around."
~Dan Millman

Sarah Ingmanson

Use your VISION to see what you would like to experience.

Is there a place you would love to visit? A concert you'd love to see? A career aspiration that enlivens you? What are those people, places, and spaces that you fail to bring to fruition simply because you haven't allowed yourself to seriously entertain them? To truly enVISION them as possible. See what happens when you take your desires seriously.

"More and more the things we could experience but become lost to us because they are banished by our failure to imagine them." ~Rainer Maria Rilke

Adjust your VISION accordingly.

We become so scared of missing our mark the first time out, but we don't know what we don't know until we "miss". It's natural to misstep when learning to walk or when trying something new. It doesn't mean your vision is to blame. It means you are human and learning. Missing may be the greatest thing that happens to you. Learn from the miss and adjust your VISION accordingly.

"Never miss twice." ~James Clear

Word of the Week

Heal through your VISION.

If there is an area of your life or your body that is bringing you pain, tension, or unhappiness, see yourself without it. Use your VISION to heal yourself.

"If you want to create something in your life, you have to contemplate yourself as surrounded by the conditions which you would like to see in your life." ~Wayne Dyer

Expand your VISION with an active imagination.

Don't "keep it real". What we know is only what we've read or experienced or heard from others. We can set rigid limits within our rigid expectations. Use your imagination to see further.

"Your imagination is more important than knowledge. For knowledge is limited to all we know and understand while your imagination embraces the entire world and all there is to know and understand." ~Albert Einstein

Sarah Ingmanson

Bring VISION to the process.

Be strategic. Create a vision board to help you stay on course. Close your eyes and see yourself there. Connect the vision in your mind to the steps you take, the conversations you initiate... the space you create for yourself and your vision to marinate.

"...the power of a vision keeps the process on track." ~Marianne Williamson

Appreciate your VISION.

Nervousness holds the same energy as excitement. Depending on whether love or fear dominates our mindset, we choose which feeling we experience. See the bigger picture value of holding a vision. A desire that is taking shape. A pulling force in your life.

"It's the possibility of having a dream come true that makes life interesting."
~Paulo Coelho

DIGNITY

Your greatness awaits... DIGNITY

We need dignity to move through sacrifice, pain, love, and failure. We aren't worthy from winning or unworthy from losing, we are worthy for reaching.

"If you go through those four things... then success is in your path and greatness is available to you." ~Jerome Bettis

Beckon dignity. Step into your greatness.

Dignity walks the walk that funds your future and fulfills your life.

"It takes 20 years to build a reputation and five minutes to ruin it. If you think about that, you'll do things differently." ~Warren Buffett

Dignity in your diet, regimen, recovery is... not complaining about it. Complaining about eating or having to do things a certain way to get the results you want is not helpful... and is certainly not dignified. When we feel acceptance and gratitude for our chosen path, our bodies release resentment and resistance, and respond more quickly.

Dignity is not enticed by... short-cuts, gimmicks, or indecent proposals. Dignity honors the process and everyone involved, and does the right thing even when no one is looking.

Dignity doesn't slack... even when the odds are stacked in your favor. Say you're up by three touchdowns, a dignified player doesn't try to rub it in through silly antics or lazy plays. Double-digit lead, crowd favorite, first callouts, no playoff implications... no matter. Act as if the outcome is not guaranteed and play your heart out. Dignity is a choice we make out of respect for our opponent, the endeavor... and for whomever gifted us with their presence today.

"There is always some kid who may be seeing me for the first time. I owe him my best."~Joe DiMaggio

DIGNITY looks a certain way.

Chin up, shoulders back... abs engaged. Forward-thinking, forward-looking, forward-being. Before, during, and after your losses *and* your wins. There is neither wallowing in defeat nor basking in glory. In your body, think about your posture, alignment, breath, precision of movement. Realize that with more dignified shapes in our body, we get *more*... with better range of motion, greater targeting of the desired muscle group, stronger core recruitment, higher caloric expenditure, improved detoxification and metabolism... and *less*... with fewer injuries.

DIGNITY feels a certain way.

Go with the flow with grace and acceptance, enjoying these final weeks of summer (or wherever you are in the year...) without losing your dignity! Find balance so as to not sabotage your goals and vision, but rather, to revitalize them.

Bring the dignity of reverence to your meals... savor each bite, buy fresh seasonal ingredients, use pretty plates, dine outside.

Dignity in your relationships is... loving yourself enough not to lose yourself.

"One's dignity may be assaulted, vandalized and cruelly mocked, but it cannot be taken away unless it is surrendered."~Morton Kondrake

Word of the Week

DIGNITY acts a certain way.

Dignity in the workplace is… helping out when your boss isn't around. You're not looking for credit, you're asking to be of service. Maybe you're doing what you know needs to be done. Or maybe you're going above and beyond the job requirement. The point is you care and you show it.

Dignity is acting like an owner… especially when you're not the owner.

"Dignity does not consist in possessing honors, but in the consciousness that we deserve them." ~ Aristotle

DIGNITY connects a certain way.

Dignity is good energy. Whether there's one person in the room or a hundred, whether it's your only class or meeting of the week or your twentieth, you act the same way. You contribute to the collective energy. Turn off your cell phone, give a smile of encouragement to the person next to you, and check your baggage at the door. See how others show up… when you do.

"Treating others with fairness and dignity is the 'rain' that helps them to grow and be more fruitful." ~ Unknown

Dignity involves listening to your heart, to living your inner truth, to knowing that it is always possible to move with dignity.

Sarah Ingmanson

Who in your life has shown you what dignity means?

DIGNITY communicates a certain way.

Dignity is our ability to know and express the truth despite what our physical eyes may be revealing (or deceiving). Maintain dignity in everything you do... take the time to make each step... each word... clean and defined.

What words or images come to mind when you hear the word, dignity?

"What people regard as vanity—leaving great works, having children, acting in such a way as to prevent one's name from being forgotten—I regard as the highest expression of human dignity." ~Paulo Coelho

DIGNITY returns a certain way.

Word of the Week

Dignity is role modeling the behavior you would like to receive. It's not what you say, but what you do that is so closely emulated.

Looking back, how have you seen dignity rewarded in others?

Looking forward, how do you see the dignity you are creating today influencing your future?

DIGNITY contemplates a certain way.

Dignity realizes… losing may be more advantageous than winning in the long run. Our biggest breakthroughs often come after our darkest days. Learning is always available. Whether we are open to learning is a decision we make for ourselves… our future selves.

Recall a time in your life when you acted with dignity, even though it was tough to. How did that make you feel before, during, and after… and now?

"It's difficult to fly freely if you have never experienced a fall. Dignity is when you can stand up, brush yourself off, and launch into a fresh new flight."
~willPower & grace

VIRTUE

Write your eulogy... VIRTUE

While our resume lists out all of the things we have achieved—the positions, the titles, our degrees and prizes, our eulogy describes who we are when those titles, awards, degrees and prizes have been stripped away.

Our eulogy will describe our virtues.

Our virtues embody how we serve and, ultimately, how we will be remembered. What will your legacy be? You need look no further than virtue.

Virtues aren't something we're born with, they are something we grow into through life experience, habit, and emulation. Most critically, they are fortified through dedicated practice.

Ultimately, we are what we repeatedly practice.

Whether we're at the gym, a restaurant, in our workplace or our homes, we assimilate what we repeatedly practice in all areas of our lives. Generosity, courage, and patience are cultivated no differently than strength, stamina, and flexibility—through dedicated practice.

We never practice in isolation either. Our habits of behavior affect our children, our colleagues, and our communities. As Jim Rohn says, we are the average of the five people we spend the most time with... so, I say invest wisely! Just as the ability to hold a 10-minute plank is a result of

Word of the Week

endurance training that inspires the person planking next to you or the person in your virtual community, our virtues are the result of a type of endurance training that both strengthen us and the human collective.

Think of it as karma... not the mainstream use of karma, which tends to focus on other people's pain and suffering for their misdeeds, but karma as a neutral force that is personal to your development. Karma is a law that just is—like gravity—nothing to be fearful of, but something to be extremely cognizant of. The power of your thoughts, words, intentions, and... virtues. Your body responds from here, your actions stem from here, and the effect is produced. During a season in which your life doesn't feel right, it's natural to look outward, but it is essential to look inward.

"Every action generates a force of energy that returns to us in like kind... what we sow is what we reap. And when we choose actions that bring happiness and success to others, the fruit of our karma is happiness and success." ~Chopra Center

Which virtues are you known for? Which ones are you currently practicing? Do you recognize the gift in whatever adversity or personal challenge you are experiencing?

For example, a hostile work environment may seem incredibly unfair at face value until you realize how much it is strengthening your ability to stay centered, how much it is strengthening your courage and conviction to leave and start that business you always dreamt about.

Getting spit on feels incredibly degrading in the moment, but sometimes we need degrading to make change. When we're in denial, we invite karma to show us. To show us what we really do not want. This contrast is often more powerful than the glimpse of what we do want.

I invite you to take inventory this week. Inventory of the virtues you wish to cultivate.. and the qualities you wish to release... in order to have the eulogy desired and the life intended. The truth-facing work we undertake this week will take us from vision... with our dignity intact... into virtue. Our virtue will carry us over any obstacles to fulfill our life purpose.

As you peruse the quotes I have selected below, you will see there is considerable debate over which virtue is the most important. It's entirely personal… personal to your life right now. Certain virtues will jump out at you as the most important to cultivate for your current situation. Which one(s) speak to you? Share with a trusted ally. Telling someone sets things in motion more quickly.

"A virtuous character is the fruit of self-discipline and good habits. (Good habits are difficult to form, but easy to live with. Bad habits are easy to form, but difficult to live with.)" ~David Tuffley

We are what we repeatedly do. Are there certain habits or routines that have grown stale, stagnant, or destructive? Take inventory and set an intention here.

Word of the Week

"The first virtue in a soldier is endurance of fatigue; courage is only the second virtue." ~Napoleon Bonaparte

Staying after the mood has left is important in creating change and staying accountable to our dreams. Fatigue is inevitable. The question is how do you endure it? How could you endure it better? Is your approach sustainable? Do you reward yourself after the "battle" is over? And, is that reward helping you recover in the direction of your dreams or taking you two steps back?

"Self respect is the cornerstone of all virtue." ~John Herschel

We don't need to do or prove anything to gain respect, but we can move from a place of self-respect. It feels different. Try it out. Know your worthiness.

"A thankful heart is not only the greatest virtue, but the parent of all other virtues." ~Cicero

Gratitude can fill the darkest corners with light. The darkest corners of ourselves. From that place of gratitude, we activate our heart to bring us out of the shadows we have created in fear back into the light of love.

"Patience is a virtue. The moon and the sun learned long ago that, if each patiently waits its turn, they will both have their chance to shine." ~Unknown

Be patient with your creativity. Pause to notice the sun and the moon. Trust that your creativity will return just as the sun and moon return to the sky or from behind the clouds.

Word of the Week

"Courage: the most important of all the virtues because without courage, you can't practice any other virtue consistently." ~Maya Angelou

The courage to see beyond what-is. The courage to trust your intuition. The courage to stop looking back. The courage to never return to the places and spaces you've outgrown. The courage to keep the current play moving forward.

"Love is the virtue of the heart, sincerity is the virtue of the mind, decision is the virtue of the will, courage is the virtue of the spirit." ~Frank Lloyd Wright

You are the sum of all your virtues. See the beauty and interplay of them in your life.

INTEGRITY

Honor yourself... INTEGRITY

Imagine you are starring in your own reality TV show. Would you change any of your behaviors, words, or actions?

On your last conference call, were you giving as much attention to the conversation as you would have had it been on video conference or in a face-to-face environment?

In a fitness class, would you brace your midsection a little more tightly if the instructor walked around and prodded at it?

If you answered yes to any of these (and, I hope you did...) then, integrity is going to be a fantastic opportunity for you (and me) to strengthen our willPower and to honor ourselves.

At the heart of integrity is self-honor.

Integrity is most commonly defined as doing the right thing from an ethical and moral standpoint. The majority of you reading this definition, is thinking:

"Duh, of course, that's common sense..."

And:

"...that's not me."

Word of the Week

Left there, we jump to the conclusion that this week's word is only relevant for Celebrity X experiencing Scandal Y. Hang on. Integrity goes beyond doing what's "right" from a legal, moral, and ethical standpoint; integrity involves doing what's "right" by our personal codes and values.

"A genius is the one most like himself." ~Thelonius Monk

Most like yourself. Your integrity is rooted in your wholeness. From the word, *integer,* meaning a whole number, a complete entity, integrity arises when you appear whole and complete.

A lack of integrity most commonly results from hiding the parts of ourselves that we dislike... the parts of ourselves that make us human. These parts tend to rear their ugly heads at the worst possible moment and in a way much less palatable than they would had we had allowed them to speak to us... through us... and into healing.

Perfectionism masks a self-worth issue. Excellence, on the other hand, evokes your willPower. Know the difference. Explore the difference... because your integrity hinges on it. Integrity can be applied in every area of our lives. Train with it. Move with it. Speak with it. Seek wholeness in yourself. Your willPower depends on it.

INTEGRITY is sticking to your set of values even when it's uncomfortable, inconvenient, painful, or problematic.

The battle becomes one within yourself. We resist change, difficult conversations, and life out of our comfort zone. It's natural, but we must move past this inner resistance to stay cloaked in our integrity.

While INTEGRITY in the gym is commonly thought of as not cheating on an exercise or an effort, it also means being honest with yourself.

Understand your motivation and intentions. When fitness becomes a form of punishment and you start treating yourself as a machine or a bad child, you lack integrity... for yourself.

INTEGRITY in your craft or career means being dedicated to quality service.

Word of the Week

This is a service to your future self. We never know how today's quality service will pay off in future opportunity or profit.

INTEGRITY *can* mean becoming a whistle blower.

As an employee, member or representative of of an organization or cause, we become part of the collective eyes and ears, and this is part of our responsibility. When it is not any of our business, though, step away.

INTEGRITY may mean having a difficult conversation or making an intervention.

Integrity doesn't permit rudeness, judgement, or jumping to conclusions, though. Integrity comes from the heart with the purest of intentions.

INTEGRITY knows the difference between doing the right thing and finding fault in others as a pastime.

This "pastime" is a diversion technique from one's own wounds and areas of personal growth. Avoidance.

INTEGRITY is doing what you say you're going to do…

Even after the initial excitement has faded… or an obstacle appears… or you're just not in the mood.

INTEGRITY is primarily an internal focus.

We ask ourselves, "Am *I* living out my values?" (Not "Is so-and-so living out *my* values?!") Integrity is not concerning yourself in what others are doing… unless it *is* your business.

INTEGRITY is more than just showing up, it's showing up "full".

While "showing up" on a consistent basis is equated with dedication and eventual success, showing up full captures the essence of integrity and elicits a superior outcome… always. It brings a better you to the table. Showing up full communicates the message to the world that you are eyes wide open alive and ready.

FAITH

Flex your spiritual willPower muscle... FAITH

"Faith doesn't make sense. That's why it makes miracles."
~John Di Lemme

Faith is part of the surrender we need to manifest our desires. Faith is the mechanism through which we remain calmly centered no matter the level of uncertainty or lack of clarity. Faith overcome fears. Faith is, literally, our spiritual willPower.

But, where dose faith comes from? Are our faith reserves dependent on how often we go to church or how long we sit in meditation? Is it related to what we eat or whether we lost two pounds this week or gained five? Is there faith correlation with the frequency of our gym check-in's or our personal plank record?

The answers are *yes* and *no*. Yes, because faith can be activated in various settings. No, because faith depends on our perspective. Although our eyes may reveal the same view, situation, or scene, our perspective dictates how we relate to it. Faith enlivens under intention and response. *Why* and *how* are more important than *what* when it comes to our actions.

Faith is an invisible force that beckons synchronicity. Faith fuels our willPower even when our engines sputter. To strengthen our willPower, we need to find and flex our faith muscle. This week, work ardently to choose faith. And, keep choosing it. Over and over. Make it your personal modus operandi and watch your life transform before your eyes.

FAITH is experienced as... an inner knowing.

Connect to the essence of who you are and the power of your connections. Trust your Warrior instincts. Notice synchronicity when it shows up in your life. Expand it by acknowledging it. The Universe is waiting for your cues.

FAITH allows you to... rest and thrive during periods of uncertainty.

Ground yourself through soft knees, drawing your belly in toward your spine, and allowing your neck to rock side to side slowly. Repeat to yourself, "I am loved" because you are so loved.

FAITH introduces... hope into the equation of our current experience.

Budget the faith multiplier in your top line. Endeavor toward increasing it over time just as you would grow your business or enhance your practice.

FAITH forms... within a peaceful mind and a soft heart.

Breathe, stretch, close your eyes, and envision yourself at your most peaceful. Where would that be? Hone in on the expression on your face.

Word of the Week

FAITH releases you from... fear.

Understand that fear is the thing that keeps you from living large and from living out your dreams. We limit ourselves through thought. The prison in your mind is literally only in your mind. Turn off the TV or any other types of channels or conversations showing you limitation you don't wish to experience.

FAITH is easier... to summon from positive experience, deliberate observation, and frequent recognition.

In the predawn hours, I look to the Eastern corner of my balcony expectantly for the telltale shades of color and light from the impending sunrise. In acknowledging our faith in any form of light, we invite faith and light into the core of our being.

Sarah Ingmanson

FAITH embraces… uncertainty.

When faced with uncertainty, shift from feeling overwhelmed to feeling curious. With faith, we can move forward with the collaborative forces. When overwhelmed, we become paralyzed and stuck within anxiety.

REMEMBER

Look both ways... REMEMBER

Remember to look both ways before crossing the street.

Remember to fasten your seat belt.

Remember to say please & thank you.

Remember to do your homework.

Remember to close the fridge.

Remember to make your bed.

Remember to set your alarm.

Remember to... eat.

Remember...9/11.

What do you REMEMBER from your childhood? What are the key "Remember..." commands that are deeply ingrained in your psyche (as in, thanks, Mom!), your digestive cues (as in a growling tummy), or in your pain body (as in, traumatic events)? Which ones are you passing down to the next generation?

We may not be able to choose what we remember, but we can choose how we remember. Ask yourself, "Is this memory serving or enslaving me?" "Is this memory softening my heart or making it rigid?" You see, what we dwell upon, dwells in us.

"Remember, you can't reach what's in front of you until you let go of what's behind you."~Unknown

This week, see how you can use your memories to propel you toward your goals... not away from them. Look both ways before crossing the next street on your journey.

REMEMBER the season.

Fall in (love). Fall out of (fear). Find familiarity in the seasonal change to the air, the routine, the fruit selection... and the sports lineup. Don the hoodie (unless it's still triple-digits where you live!)

REMEMBER to breathe.

This might sound strange like a strange command at face value, but conscious breath improves the exercise, the meditation, the experience... no matter whether you are sitting at your desk, in traffic, or in a wall sit (a challenging exercise hold). Try it now... breathe in deeply through your nose and exhale slowly as you consciously tighten your midsection. (Yes, forget the waist-trainer. Bracing while exhaling is much more effective at "training" your waistline!)

REMEMBER you can't outrun (or out waist-train) your fork.

Nutrition is at least 80% of the fitness equation. If you are serious about fitness, you must be serious about your nutrition.

REMEMBER to align fitness to your lifestyle.

When fitness becomes misaligned, it becomes just another obligation or optional activity in your life, which can invite guilt or shame. Reframe your to-do list. Symbolically link these items to your dream or vision.

REMEMBER to acknowledge and appreciate the completion of each mini-milestone.

Otherwise there will be no joy in achieving.

REMEMBER that some things cannot hurt you anymore unless you invite them back in through thought and memory.

Pay attention to triggers and self-imposed limitations, guilt, shame, or punishment resulting from memory and the subconscious mind.

REMEMBER that fitness is an expedition, requiring great awareness and a healthy mind, body, and spirit.

Seek balance between the three to energize your trajectory.

REMEMBER in plank.

Dedicate your plank to courageous acts of willPower and the heroes in your life… or in your memory. Your practice of willPower spills over to all areas of your life, strengthening you for the everyday… and the not-so-everyday… challenges.

REMEMBER your avatar.

Word of the Week

An avatar could be your ideal client, the person you are trying to reach in your service to the world... whether it's through spreadsheets, sales, or salon. An avatar can also be thought of as part of your soul group.... your tribe. People who see the world similarly to you.

REMEMBER there is human tragedy, but also remember our unique role and responsibility not to proliferate tragedy.

That means by not inviting it in through fear, hatred, judgement, or other negative thought patterns.

REMEMBER that song?

Mix up the playlist. Get nostalgic. Revisit some songs from your childhood or different periods of your life. Watch how it spurs your creative mind.

REMEMBER to use your senses.

Slow down the racing thinking mind by consciously turning up your sensory mind to presently see, listen, smell, touch, taste. Did you know that scents stir the most memory of all?

REMEMBER why the goal is important to you.

Connect the goal to your vision. When you remember the context, you'll stay happier and committed.

REMEMBER it's the journey that creates your most treasured moments; not one day or one finish line.

It's who you have become in the process that is the gift to yourself.

REMEMBER a time that you rose to the occasion and discovered strength you didn't know you possessed.

Reflecting back on that event or situation vividly, notice how your current attitude, perspective, and energy shifts.

REMEMBER your lessons as you release the pain from your past... and our collective past.

DEPTH

Go a mile deep... DEPTH

The temptation is to go wide rather than deep... to know a little about everything... to wander off into tangents, and to allow our inbox to guide us to this task or that response. We gain more value and life-satisfying purpose, though, from identifying our niche and going deep. Seek to become an expert... a person of value... someone of DEPTH.

This week, I invite you to go a mile deep. Go to the edge of your comfort zone.... and then a little beyond. Find your depth. It's life-generating. In our depth, we learn more about ourselves... what we're made of... what we can endure. From this place of depth, we then come to know and understand our true power... ahem, our willPower.

Find DEPTH in your (Warrior) pose.

Word of the Week

Go deep into your body. Find the edge of your pose. Go one inch deeper in your squat. Stay deep and hold until the muscle starts to shake.

Massage deeply. Use your thumbs along the landing pad of your foot. Use your knuckles along the transverse arch of your foot. Work out the adhesions.

"Hidden beneath your feet is a luminous stage where you are meant to rehearse your eternal dance." ~Hafiz

Find the DEPTH in your desire.

The depth of your desire cultivates the level of your inspiration. Which activities, causes, or pastimes are you most passionate about? If you had the time, money, (insert other limiting factor holding you back), what would do... or do more of?

Sarah Ingmanson

Cultivate your DEPTH in mastery.

For the athlete, depth brings mastery. No matter what your "sport" is—gardening, teaching, parenting, dancing, photography, bodybuilding, etc., mastery delivers a unique vision and a sense of fulfillment from deepening your practice.

"Mastery... to know a certain domain of the world in depth... the inevitable result of sustained concentration of an object of intense interest."~Stephen Cope

Expand your DEPTH through your breath.

Practice deep heart-centered breathing. Close your eyes. Feel your heart expanding with your inhale. Let go of any deep hurts with your exhale.

Word of the Week

"In the depth of winter, I finally learned that there was in me an invincible summer." ~Albert Camus

Retreat into your DEPTH.

Go deep into a retreat... formally or informally. My in-flight entertainment is usually a book or a notebook. In a quiet space above the clouds, the ideas seem to roll in with fluidity and easy. Even if you don't have a long trans-Pacific flight halfway around the world, take some time to journal a little more deeply about what is going on *in* your world. Clear away the blockages. Allow your inspiration to flow through you as it was meant to.

"There is a vitality, a life force, an energy, a quickening that is translated through you into action, and because there is only one of you in all of time, this expression is unique. And if you block it, it will never exist through any other medium and it will be lost. The world will not have it. It is not your business to determine how good it is nor how valuable nor how it compares with other expressions. It is your business to keep it yours clearly and directly, to keep the channel open." ~Martha Graham

Sarah Ingmanson

Invite DEPTH into your learning.

Study something in-depth. Just as our bodies need nutrients and exercise, our minds need knowledge and inspiration for vitality. Books have a power to create a mini-world within us. That depth is restorative to our souls.

"Knowledge is only a rumor until it is in the muscle." ~New Guinea proverb

Discover your personal DEPTH.

Explore beneath the surface and find greater depth. By drilling down into the depths of something, you discover your own depths. As you go to sleep, set the intention to rest more deeply. Keep a notebook by your bed to jot down any dreams upon awakening.

"Examine each fiber. Persist in your quest. Squeeze harder and engage more fully. Think it through completely; from all angles, and understand it all. Be fully you; to the very depth of your soul." ~willPower & grace

CHANGE

Roll with it... CHANGE

"The only thing constant is change." ~Heraclitus

When change strikes, the tendency to play victim is compelling. After all, we can rationalize, "I did nothing to bring this about..." But, the victim role drains our energy as we fixate on past circumstances and stay stuck in a "woe is me" energy pattern. An empowered response accepts that we did play a role in bringing this about—consciously or unconsciously. By setting intentions and holding a vision strongly in our mind's eye, the Universe begins to set things in motion, very much conspiring on our behalf.

We resist change and cling to what is gone because "what is gone" was comfortable at some level. We knew what to expect... maybe we thought things couldn't get better (especially not like this!)... or we believed that our current path must be the best one.

Yet, by accepting and rolling with change, we can free ourselves from the useless energy expended in "clinging" to the past. We set ourselves free to explore and align with what lies ahead under this new set of parameters.

"All the buried seeds crack open in the dark the instant they surrender to a process they cannot see." ~Mark Nepo

Seeking the concrete and static, we become concrete and static... that is, in our growth potential and our vision. We allow ourselves to be weighed down by the fears and insecurities behind our clinging for control of the uncontrollable. When we show an eagerness to roll with the punches, a confidence that our skillset is strong, adaptive, and flexible, and a vision to see the silver lining in our changing circumstances, the Universe goes to divine bat for us.

"Without change, something sleeps inside us, and seldom awakens. The sleeper must awaken." ~Frank Herbert, author

When I was nearing the end of business school, I was tossing around the idea of pursuing a PhD and a career in academia. On my list of pros & cons, I had written down stability and job security as key "pros". I expected my advisor, herself a tenured professor at a prestigious university, to nod her head emphatically and welcome me with open arms to "her world". Instead, she shook her head and said,

"Sarah, it doesn't work that way. No matter which line of work you pursue, you will need to constantly evolve to stay on the top of your game." ~Professor Olivia Mitchell

In other words, no profession would grant me a magical passage to easy street where I could simply relax and work on autopilot. Nor would I want it to... As uncomfortable as change can be, we all need that proverbial kick in the rear to accept personal responsibility, to keep reinventing ourselves, and to continue to grow.

"If you think adventure is dangerous, try routine. It is lethal." ~Paulo Coelho

Change can feel disruptive, unexpected, and unnerving... or it can feel liberating, transformative, and exciting beyond our wildest dreams. It's a decision only we can make... as life unfolds right in front of us.

"Whether the reality of change is a source of freedom for us or a source of horrific anxiety makes a significant difference." ~Pema Chodron

CHANGE at the densest level.

We stand in awe when we see a martial artist chop a wooden block with his bare hand because any change to the physical nature of something takes deliberate mental focus and an unwavering belief. The saying, "abs are made in the kitchen" is true in the sense that what happens "in the kitchen" results from all the little choices we make throughout the day, week, and year. When our commitment and self-love dips, so does our willPower. But, if we realize "the statue already exists within the marble", we can stay loving to ourselves while removing the excess marble...

"I saw the angel in the marble and I chiseled until I set it free." ~Michelangelo

Changing our bodies is inherently difficult because we are changing something at the densest energy level. Dig deeper in your self-awareness to respond to the signals in your changing body, appetite, and energy levels, without getting caught up in the what-used-to-be's or the uncomfortable extremes of craving and aversion.

Word of the Week

CHANGE the intention.

When we engage in any type of change mission, we are looking to "birth" something out of unconditional love. We can birth it the other way—out of self-hatred, shame, or for external validation, but that backfires as we end up giving away our power and self-worth in the process.

When motivation or intention is externally-focused, changes stay up near the surface. Underneath, we find layers of pain, insecurity, and fear buried, and these layers expose us to self-sabotage and reversion to old destructive patterns.

CHANGE the attitude.

If it doesn't come from within you, it will go without you.

If we infuse our personal journeys with a "yeah, but ____" mentality, we dilute our focus and provide an easy scapegoat to aim low. Alternatively, we can open our eyes to how our unique circumstances will help us succeed in a way that we've never been able to succeed before.

Work to keep your "Yeah, but ____" thoughts from drifting off to self-diminishing conclusions of hardship and subpar outcomes. Finish the thought instead by affirming to yourself "so I can know how to manifest this out of unconditional love."

Embrace the CHANGE.

"Love thy neighbor. Ignore thy neighbor." ~Barre3

Self-love isn't about seeing yourself as better than anyone else or proving to the world you're smarter, more beautiful, wealthier, stronger... or in any other way more worthy of love and admiration. This is about loving all your parts so you don't need any of that... and so you can invite others to do the same.

New boss at work? New colleague... new management or directional shift in something you're doing? How can you mesh with this change to bring out your best?

Word of the Week

"Be the change that you wish to see in the world." ~Mahatma Gandhi

Speak CHANGE.

Change cultivates our aliveness, enhances our vitality, and summons our intuition. I always write more when I am traveling, which reminds me I should change scenery more often. We all should. Endure the hassle, the inconvenience, and the expense of change when you can. Away from familiar territory is where we have the opportunity to change the most. So, step out. Step up. Create change around you, about you… and, most especially, over you. Change is in the air… especially when you *change* the air.

CHANGE your perception.

So much of our lives relate to our perception. Where you see tragedy, another may see opportunity. Where you see suffering, another may see hope. Don't underestimate the impact your perception has on your reality.

"A miracle is just a shift in perception." ~Marianne Williamson

Foster CHANGE.

Change brings challenge and uncertainty, but also an air of anticipation and excitement—a welcome and different energy altogether. What can you change in your mind or in your world to further your dreams and desires?

PEACE

Generate an even harmony... PEACE

Whether you are building a baby, a body, a company, or any other dream, change emerges and it is our ability to shift that keeps us at peace within ourselves and in a generative consciousness.

gen·er·a·tive (adj) relating to or capable of production or reproduction.

"If it's something you're really serious about, it's necessary not to take it too seriously... To be generative, you cannot be only serious. You've got to be able to play." ~Robert Dilts

Serious, but not too serious because playfulness fosters creativity, different perspectives, and new possibilities for greater joy. Without playfulness, we get stuck in a really bad place... misery.

"If peace comes from seeing the whole, then misery comes from a loss of perspective." ~ Mark Nepo

See the whole. Admire the view. Find something to appreciate and allow that place of gratitude soothe you into peace. In Japanese, the two kanji characters that combine to make peace are 平和, *heiwa*, literally meaning an "even harmony".

This week, as you harmonize with peace, think about creating an even harmony through all of your chakra archetypes. What would these look like? And, more importantly, what would they feel like?

Sarah Ingmanson

Cultivate internal PEACE within your body.

A peaceful body digests faster and operates more efficiently. Allow your unproductive thoughts and worries subside as you set out on your day. Eat foods that your body processes well and supports a peaceful belly. For example, add lemon to your water to alkalize your body. Although lemons are an acidic fruit, they have an alkalizing effect upon the body. It is the mineral composition of the fruit that matters and, in the lemon's case, that causes the body to become more alkaline when the lemon is metabolized. When our bodies are more alkaline, the oxygenation of the blood is increased, which provides extra energy and health improvements.

"A Warrior of the Light is not constantly repeating the same struggle, especially when there are neither advances nor retreats." ~Paulo Coelho

Let PEACE anchor you.

The emotional opposite of peace is rage, so seek times to find peace throughout your day... times when minor irritants might turn into full-blown rage if left to fester. Put out the fire with your peaceful intent... and perhaps a few deep breaths! The peace comes from the pause. Use that pause to regain your peaceful center. Be playful when it's safe and appropriate to do so. Let laughter provide you with that even harmony of "serious, but not too serious".

Surround yourself in PEACE.

How can you make your workouts more peaceful this week? Maybe take a quiet jog outside and enjoy the sunrise. Leave the MP3 at home if you can jog someplace peaceful... or adjust the musical selection to more peaceful chords if you need to block out a noisy environment. A tight body is never a peaceful one. This would be a great week to cultivate your yoga practice. Or, just dedicate some time to forward folds, letting your upper body hang forward and shaking your head slowly from side to side to release your neck.

Sarah Ingmanson

Bring PEACE with you.

Be mindful of shared space. Are you yapping on your phone while others are in close proximity. Could you wait to take that phone call in the privacy of your office, car, or home? Is there tension in any of your relationships that you could alleviate with a gesture of peace? Start small. This isn't about caving in. This is about creating a peaceful presence in yourself. Notice how others respond to you. Notice what or who shows up in your life when you're rocking a peaceful vibe.

Create in PEACE.

Is your creative work space peaceful? What would enhance the peaceful elements? Introduce a little "spa" into your space. Aromatherapy sprays are an easy way to infuse the air with a peaceful scent. A mug of hot herbal tea works as well. Is there clutter in your workspace that is diminishing your peace? Are there a few things on your to-do list

Word of the Week

that have been nagging you for way too long? Maybe this would be a good day to cross one of those off... in the interest of your peace.

Visualize PEACE.

Close your eyes and envision yourself at your most peaceful. What would that look like? Where would you be? What would you be wearing? Memorize the expression on your face. As you go through your day, try to bring that feeling into being. Pause and return to your vision as often as needed. Use visual or audio cues to remind you to return.

Sarah Ingmanson

Recognize and emulate PEACE.

Who is your role model for peace? How is your life's work… purpose… dharma connected to peace? As you strengthen your peace within, acknowledge how it influences your thought patterns, behaviors, and outcomes.

PATIENCE

Incubating in.... PATIENCE (Week 1)

Anything with an incubation period invites both love and fearful speculation, tempting us to go "out of order" in hiding our fear and attempting to control things we simply cannot. There's an alternative, of course. We can protect our minds, practice patience, and actively commit to staying anchored to this present moment:

While seeking PATIENCE this week (*and* next), actively release whatever doesn't serve you and your dreams. Notice when the following queries, statements, or thoughts show up in conversation or inner dialogue this week:

1. When will you _____?
2. Are you sure it's safe to _____?
3. You better _____.
4. Watch out for _____.
5. So, does this mean _____?
6. What if _____?

Although well-intentioned and seemingly harmless, these questions and commentary all contain elements of limitation, fear, or future expectation, enticing us into a controlling mindset and living out someone else's experience of life.

We often live as if we are in control over our own lives and destiny. We will do just about anything to maintain an illusion of control. To feel powerful and in control, we act out and do things that give us a semblance of control.

We think, "I can't surrender, I can't let go... all hell will break loose." But, it is the opposite—the armor we put on, the forcing and resisting, the pushing and pulling—that's when hell really breaks loose.

In the spirit of being fully present in patience, here is our "let-go" list for the week:

Cravings

Appreciate your cravings as internal wisdom from your body or a temporary adjustment to a new meal plan. Cravings can signal deficiencies, hormonal imbalance, or resistance to change. This is why cravings are prevalent during pregnancy, a certain time of the month, or when on an extreme diet. If there is no health issue or concern, acknowledge the cravings in healthy, mindful ways that support your goal.

Word of the Week

How this will play out

Patience is closely linked to trust. When we trust, we find it easier to be patient. So, trust. Today is a day to celebrate; a new day we've never experienced before. Relax and enjoy this day as much as possible. Your body responds to everything you think and feel.

The need to be better or perfect

Stop demanding perfection from yourself (or anyone else) and just be perfectly in the moment. Allow yourself to have mediocre training days. Recognize progress is not always linear. In fact, it rarely is.

The annoying elements

Infuse your situation with love, gratitude, and patience for all the elements… even the annoying ones!

Complaints

Whatever your current ailment or frustration is, the more you complain, the more you will feed your inner and outer turmoil.

Future scenarios

There is a time and a place for scenario planning. Carve it out deliberately. If you are unable to shake the anxious thoughts, go workout. Exercise is the best remedy for any kind of mental or emotional stress.

Keeping score

Tit for tat retaliation or zero-sum thinking keeps us in a ping-pong game of life. That is, constantly reacting, defending, and battling. By letting go of the scorecard, we can bring more patience into the unfolding. Instead of wasting our time keeping score, scheming how we will get even, suspecting malicious intent, or greedily securing our share of the pie, we sit back and allow the negative energy to pass over us. Never to touch us. In patience, we stay grounded in our worthiness, living out our dharma, and honoring our intent to lead a soul-satisfying life.

PATIENCE

Deja vu... PATIENCE (Week 2)

We practice patience when we give up attachments to results. Not because they don't matter, but because they matter so much. We want the things to happen in life that benefit us the most. We can rest in knowing that if we do ultimately belong to this career, this relationship, this lifestyle, this location... we absolutely will get there... because our hearts will guide us to it.

Take a moment and recognize the role that control or fear plays in your life. Have you already decided what you think your future "should" bring? (Or what it better *not* bring?!) Have things ever worked out differently in your life and, in hindsight, you see they worked out better than what you had pre-conceived?

This week, the challenge is to go the softer patient way. Discover it is actually your strength. Be fully invested in the effort for the sake of being fully invested in an effort. Show up in excellence, integrity, contribution, and give it all you've got with no guarantee of where it's going... knowing that when you patiently stand up in your excellence, it is going somewhere.

Word of the Week

"The embryo doesn't need to visualize to become a baby." ~Marianne Williamson

With PATIENCE, we can trust in our innate abilities to grow and strengthen even without visual proof.

"Grasping for the impossible (total control) is the root of addictions." ~Michelle Margaret

With PATIENCE, let go of the need to micro-manage or control every element. Lose the addictive mindset and relax into the possible.

"Patience is full of empathy—so it has the power to change you, as well as those around you. As you practice patience—with yourself and others, heartache, discomfort and frustration move into the past. They never will have the power that they hold in the present." ~ willPower & grace

Power is self-manifested through PATIENCE. Allow painful moments of defeat dissolve into the past where they can no longer hurt you.

"Find patience with the conditions of your life, with the baggage that you must sometimes carry, and the foggy path which lies ahead. Have patience with the noise in the air, and with the people around you. Have patience with all that remains unsolved in your heart." ~willPower & grace

Word of the Week

With PATIENCE, heal your heart. Don't take everything so seriously or personally! Lighten up. Soften your heart as you heal the hardened places.

"Breathe. Let go. And remind yourself that this very moment is the only one you know you have for sure." ~Oprah Winfrey

A good exhale and a healthy shift in perspective will bring clarity back into our eyes. With PATIENCE, we shift our direction toward life-serving pursuits and appreciative thought patterns.

"All thought creates form on some level." ~ A Course in Miracles

In other words, be careful with that recurring thought in your head! You are creating something with it right now. How does that change how you think? How does that incentivize you to care about what you are thinking… and be more selective? With PATIENCE, we know our positive mindset will assist us in creating something magnificent.

"Make space for your future." ~Danielle LaPorte, *Truthbomb*

With PATIENCE, we allow the Universe to conspire in our favor. We don't rush to see or demand to know, we trust that things are working out better than we could single-handedly orchestrate or imagine.

PRECISION

Age with... PRECISION

"The way you think, the way you behave, the way you eat, can influence your life by 30 to 50 years." ~ *Deepak Chopra*

...in which case, my mom is roughly my age!

As I stood in the middle of a pack of senior line dancers, I began to pick up not only the steps, but the spoken and unspoken rules of this silver-haired dance troupe.

"We go out to lunch together frequently and always ice cream on Friday."

To move with precision as a team, socializing helps. Schedule a team-building event or just grab lunch with the new person on your team. Attend a group fitness class or any type of class where movement is coordinated. Create a connection deeper than an obligatory one.

Sarah Ingmanson

"There's something comforting in precision."

Line dancers work to stay evenly spaced and to move in unison, reminding me of my synchronized skating days... formerly known as "precision" skating.

Moving in precision is beautiful, rewarding, and neatly organized. Coordinated movement is soothing to the soul.

"We don't mind if anyone messes up."

That put me instantly at ease because it's daunting to be the newbie. You don't want to ruin it for the others (or stick out like a sore thumb). Assure the new person on your team that it's OK to ask questions… and to mess up!

"When someone doesn't show up, we call their house."

The vast majority of these seniors are widows and they provide each other with an informal support system. (Besides, think how much better you would stick to your fitness regime or New Year's Resolutions if someone were calling your house looking for you!)

Regardless of age or marital status, reach out. Let someone know you noticed their absence. They might need your help… or simply their day brightened.

"If you don't listen too closely, it's fine."

I giggled when my mother took offense at the lyrics to "Save a horse, ride a cowboy", but had no problems shaking her hips to "Blurred Lines". She acknowledged the controversy (some senior centers have even banned Robin Thicke's song) and purports to overcome any embarrassment by tuning out the lyrics. In hindsight, I realize that my mom has been perfecting the art of selective hearing for years...

Sometimes, ignorance is bliss. We can't always control the lyrics playing around us. Use selective hearing to tune out what doesn't elevate you and tune into what does.

"Come here into the center because we will face all directions."

Line dancing requires memorization as you turn to face different sides of the room without the crutch of verbal (or visual) instruction. To my surprise, there were very few mistakes... fewer than in my classes full of cueing, role modeling... and mirrors! The difference? Everyone was completely tuned in. So, regardless of anyone "minding" mistakes, the collective mindfulness was the glue reinforcing the steps, the focus, and the rhythm.

Make it your own piece of personal pride and responsibility to be "tuned in". Superior presence manifests superior mental performance.

Word of the Week

"We celebrate our birthdays.. with the correct age."

Something to keep in mind if you've been planning your "29th" birthday celebration (again and again). Facing each birthday with dread has a deleterious effect on the body a compared to celebration. Celebrate your life by taking care of yourself… with PRECISION.

TRANSFORM

Summon your inner alchemist...
TRANSFORM

To transform, we must shift... find a shift within ourselves. Shift our inner world so the outer world may respond. An outer transformation is what many of us seek. What happens inside dictates what shows up outside. To truly transform, we must think beyond skin deep.

To transform, we sustain a commitment of change in an intentional direction. To transform, we feel the shift first within ourselves. We've set our sights. The vision has formed within our minds. We listen for the right moment to move. We anticipate, but we don't move until the day arrives. The day of the event or the day we are guided to move. There is a different kind of strength associated with being able to hold a pose, to deliberately squeeze the muscles in the inner thighs, and then breathe into the squeeze. There is belief, confidence, conviction, focus, and determination symbolized in our holding and deliberate engagement. As we release the pose, we feel how our patience has paid off.

The curtain lifts, the door opens, and we are ready to arrive. Never to go back. Because we are not the same person anymore. We are transformed.

Transform means to make a thorough or dramatic change in form, appearance, or character. A room can be transformed by a fresh coat

Word of the Week

of paint or new hardwood floors. Your backyard can be transformed overnight by snowfall. Your body can be transformed as you release resentment, dis-ease, or limiting beliefs about how life is supposed to go. In medical terms, transform means to cause to change, as in to cause a cell to undergo genetic transformation. In physics, transform means to change into another form of energy.

As you go through your week, think deeply about the kind of transformation you are seeking.

Start from the ground up.

Until we feel safe and secure, we lack the stable foundation from which to grow and transform.

Elicit your desire.

How would it feel in your ideal transformed state? See yourself transformed. Feel it in every ounce of your being. Become the vibrational match to that which you desire.

Create forward motion.

Allow your personal energy to transform inertia into action and movement. What challenges can you meet today to create forward motion in your life?

Bring it into your heart.

Be grateful for the challenges that have helped you transform your fear and open up to love.

Word of the Week

Communicate as-if.

Fool yourself. When you act as-if you're already transformed, you create from that vantage point. Communicate to the Universe through your words and expressions that you are serious.

Seek answers.

Why is this time different? How did past experiences prepare you for this? What changed or clicked within you? Why does the world look differently to you now? What feels different within you?

Connect to others.

A historic figure. A fictional character in a book. The heroine. The athlete on another continent preparing for the same event. The person next to you in line who is also seeking their own personal transformation. Feel the strength of connection. We are all in this together. Past, present, and future.

EXPLORE

Leave the map behind... EXPLORE

When traveling, you quickly realize how culture is infused in every experience. Whether you are eating at a restaurant, taking the subway—or checking out a local gym, anticipate there will be spoken and unspoken rules to learn and abide by. This is part of the foreign adventure and an opportunity to be open to the new and unexpected.

To explore is to leave the map behind. The map that enables us to go on auto-pilot in our workouts, our careers, our relationships, or... all of the above... in life, in general. At some point, the maps we carry lose their inherent usefulness and turn into baggage. Whether our maps take the form of an actual map, GPS, iPhone, parental expectations, or social programming, they each have the potential to hold us back. When we rely on maps, we dull down our innate scientific tools.

"Equipped with his five senses, man explores the universe around him and calls the adventure Science." ~Edwin Hubble

This is why we explore with all five senses. Our senses provide us with information and personalize our experiences. Without our informed (exploratory) consent, life feels random and unsatisfying because we've lost some consciousness and create by default.

"Remember when your curiosity inspired your investigative mind to explore and learn... you weren't bogged down with resentment, cynicism, and

emotional baggage… just think about how great it would be to return to that mindset of unencumbered learning and adventurous living… you are just one choice away from that life… choose to let go of the infertile past… go live your adventure!"—Steve Maraboli

When we stop learning, we lose our way. This week, you will not necessarily need your passport, but you will need your five senses switched on.

Eat a meal with the intention to explore. Heighten all of your senses to fully taste and experience the meal.

Wear a texture or color to match an emotional void (e.g. your favorite sweats to feel cozy; the color green to feel loved/loving). Notice if it helps.

Change your hair, make-up, or any other aspect of your style, and let your reflection in the mirror surprise you. Does the change inspire a change in your attitude, confidence, or self-perception? Does this, in turn, change the way people treat or respond to you?

When you exercise or work, imagine you have lost one of your senses (e.g. vision) and have to rely on your other four senses exclusively.

Call or send a note to someone you haven't been in contact with for over a year. How do you feel afterwards?

Sarah Ingmanson

Turn off the music, TV, or other background noise in your home, car, office, or workout. Notice all of the sounds you have been drowning out. How does the quiet make you feel?

Leave your phone behind when you go out for a walk, a meal, or a sporting event. What do you notice when you are fully present? Even if it generates boredom. Allow it into your experience in order to accept and move past it.

Google Image a place you wish to visit, live, work, attend... then visualize yourself there. Invite it into your experience so you can magnetize yourself toward it.

Hang out with natural-born explorers... e.g. pets, babies... people on a mission. Imagine the world through their eyes. Let their vision inspire yours.

Word of the Week

Make one deliberate move each day to honor a personal dream of yours. No matter how small, let the act symbolize your conviction and draw you closer to your desired destination.

"If you appreciate, perpetuate and explore your own dreams, then you'll know that dream isn't a one-way communication." ~Toba Beta

SURRENDER

Stop, drop, and... SURRENDER

We don't surrender when it's convenient. We surrender when it seems utterly inconvenient. You know it when... there's that thing you want so badly that you have poured your heart and soul into it, you dream about it at night, you visualize the moment when you finally _____ (fill in your blank here). Are you with me? And, even better, are you there right now? If so, kindly stop, drop, and... SURRENDER.

Surrender is a choice we make... a strong choice... to do nothing. But, if you are thinking, "Do nothing, sign me up!", then, I'm afraid you are not there. (Return to above, start from 'pour heart & soul', then we'll talk...) When you want something badly, doing nothing feels like torture. It feels as if you are letting your dream slip away... but, you are not. You are manifesting it in the best of ways.

Surrender is not defeat; it is self-victory.

At first glance, the words, *surrender* and *willPower* seem to be on opposite ends of the spectrum. That happens when we confuse surrender with submission, strength with weakness, raising the flag with throwing in the towel. Surrender in a willPower sense involves stepping out of the way of ourselves and allowing the best to unfold gracefully.

"We can let our lives be directed by the same force that makes flowers grow—or we can do it ourselves." ~Marianne Williamson

Word of the Week

When we feel like our happiness, goal and/or survival hinges on others or our outer circumstances, we reclaim our willPower in the surrender. As we surrender in mind and spirit, our bodies respond with harmony and strength.

SURRENDER to discomfort.

Finish the set even if it's a struggle. Work 15 extra minutes after you decide it's time to take a break or call it a day.

SURRENDER to rest.

Yes to both. We need to balance the discomfort with sufficient rest. Rest is a key ingredient to recovery and an essential component of fitness. Look around and see the "scraped knees" and noticeable limps of those around you who have not put responsibility, discipline and mature patience into play... recognize just how fundamental surrender is for your survival.

SURRENDER an overly restrictive mindset.

Replace this with a more inclusive and moderate approach to fitness.

"A woman (or man) with a history of ED [Eating Disorders] is very likely to take the ball and run with it. If you say, "Don't eat tomatoes, they have sugar"- that client with an ED is very likely to now label tomatoes as a 'bad'

food. Which if you understand science, tomatoes are not a bad food, they can fit perfectly into any macro plan. If you tell them that 'cardio' is good, chances are very high that they will only feel accomplished if they 'cardio' every day."
~Jennifer Jewell

SURRENDER to how you feel without restraint or apology.

If you are happy, be happy. If you are sad, be sad. If you are going to laugh, laugh. If you want to cry your eyes out, do it. Think of your emotions (especially the strong intense ones...) as an internal alarm system designed to expose hidden desires, motivations, fears, and areas that require new wise action. Instead of making yourself wrong or weak, step back and get curious. What and where are these emotions asking you to pay attention? Let them lead you to the next step for growth and perseverance in the timing of things.

SURRENDER to being clumsy or looking silly.

Fear of looking silly keeps us on the sidelines... of life. Think of how a toddler plays without reservation. See the connection between playfulness and joy. Your joy awaits.

Word of the Week

SURRENDER the outer/inner critic.

Go through your social media feed and take the first post that annoys you (or, in your daily life, the first remark that gets under your skin). Surrender the criticism and look in the proverbial mirror—this is a quality you are in denial about. Otherwise, it would not give you a charge. Surrender to it and own it. Jot down, "I am…" and find a few ways to honor it in your life (without harming yourself or others… or breaking any laws!)

SURRENDER to differences in opinions.

See if you can omit these phrases in your everyday conversations, "Why did you…?", "Yes, but…" or "You should…

SURRENDER to what is.

Identify the "edge" every single day, and take care not to cross it. By surrendering with self-love, our bodies receive a strong signal to release resistance... and excess baggage. Realize that sometimes the most powerful thing you can do is surrender:

"That which is surrendered is taken care of best... To keep it ourselves means to constantly grab and clutch and manipulate. We keep opening the oven to see if the bread is baking, which only ensures that it never gets a chance to."
~Marianne Williamson

SURRENDER to a painful truth.

A good one... one that elicits feelings of resentment, anger, jealously and/or regret... a time when you were "wronged". Through surrender, we create space and awareness. By not "being" the story, we no longer have to suffer in the story. Diffuse the emotional charge and surrender to what happened.

SURRENDER to non-reaction.

When someone criticizes or blames you, try this—do nothing. Absolutely nothing. Aside from perturbing your attacker, just see how it feels. After that initial (uncomfortable) diminishment, find the spaciousness to realize that nothing real has been diminished, and that through becoming "less", you have actually become "more"... much more!

Word of the Week

SURRENDER the form of what you want.

Journal about the essence of your deepest desire instead. The essence is the manifestation. Realize the form you have in mind may not be the best form for the essence you seek. Focus on essence and journal away!

SURRENDER to what is.

Sarah Ingmanson

Many limitations can be overcome externally, but others cannot; they can only be overcome internally. You have the choice to stay trapped in an ego-centric reaction (aka intense unhappiness) or to rise above and surrender. Choose to love your limitations as the spiritual gifts they represent.

VALUE

A Slippery Slope... VALUE

Don't be fooled into thinking your neighbor... mother... or anyone knows better than you. Who is to say that price tag is expensive or cheap? You. Outside market forces and "what other people say" are just that—outside of you and not you.

When we succumb to external judgments of value, we give away our power. We fail to realize we are the ultimate value setters—based on what we uniquely perceive. We suffer when the value we perceive doesn't measure up to the price we pay. And, to help us mitigate this suffering, we have this week—a week devoted to value.

Why settle for less? Good question. We do this when we feel we need to justify the value gap we have with others. We also do this when we undervalue ourselves and don't feel worthy of the 'extravagance'.

So, when you catch yourself saying, "Yes, but I got this on sale..." or "Yes, but.... xyz", ask yourself, "What am I trying to defend?" Is it truly the price you paid or what you value? We value according to how it matters in our heart, so when you deny that value, you deny yourself. What do you value? What are you worth? What do you deserve? You see, it's a slippery slope.

Sarah Ingmanson

VALUE your body.

What we treat as valuable flourishes. Are you feeding or otherwise treating your body as valuable? What can you do to bring more high quality foods into your diet. Don't think in terms of dollar signs, think in terms of value.

VALUE what "money can't buy."

What are they for you? A beautiful view. Hand holding. A great night's sleep. Think about ways to make this valuable stuff more prominent in your life.

VALUE your space.

Word of the Week

To move, feel, be. Create some sacred space in your home just for you. Carve out a corner of your office as well. A place to meditate. A place with a few key tokens, ornaments, pictures, or symbols. A place that strengthens your sense of self-worth, value, and intention.

VALUE your strength.

When have you been strong in a way that surprised yourself? This is a powerful moment to bring into your core and to bolster your confidence in your capabilities.

VALUE your renumeration.

Do you get paid enough for what you do? If your answer is "no", realize something is 'out of whack' in either your perception or your profession. We don't have to be paid in monetary terms to feel well-compensated. Money is just one mechanism. But, there is a consciousness about it.

VALUE the environment.

We often think our individual decisions don't matter, but they do. When we honor our environment through thoughtful decisions like reusable grocery bags and sustainable investment, our environment honors us. Our world is a mirror of what we value and how we honor our value system.

Get up in the morning and engage from your heart. If it's something of VALUE, trust you will get the outcome you need.

VALUE your inner voice.

Carve out some time for quiet contemplation in your sacred space. If meditation is not your thing, find something that works—cooking, painting, coloring, writing, walking in nature, planking…

Word of the Week

VALUE your time.

Take stock of the disconnect between what you value and where you are spending your time. Time is a larger determinant of happiness than money. But, we often spend our time blindly. So, bring awareness and intention to your time allocation.

VALUE your intuition even when it runs contrary to conventional thinking or the so-called "expert" opinion.

VALUE your talent.

Think about your unique talent. How is it valued? What are ways you can tap into that talent to cultivate it further, to increase your intrinsic value, and to, ultimately, enhance your 'net worth'?

VALUE your dreams.

Get real. What are they? And, why aren't you going for them? Year-end is a natural time for reflection. Forget early Christmas shopping, try early Dream shopping...

GRATITUDE

Gratitude... where life happens better.

I was terrified of gymnastics week in gym class. Amazingly, now my favorite pose is... the backbend. Apparently, for good reason, too. Do you know that backbends massage and exercise the heart in much the same way that running does? In backbend, the upper quads are engaged to push the pelvis forward while muscles in the feet and hamstrings strengthen the hips, legs and lower back. By moving the spine both forward and backward, the heart is stretched in many directions... just like in gratitude.

Do you spend more time thinking about what you do have or what you don't have? Is that proverbial glass half-full or half-empty? If it is half-empty, why don't you fill it? Fill it conceptually (if not, actually...). Once we treat it as a choice, we become accountable. We do things that fill us... and, more importantly, we stop doing the things that leave us empty. There is absolute perfection in our imperfection and light in our darkness. We are gifted with a vision that sees through darkness and brings us back to light.

Where the gratitude hits the road, we find true comfort. Gratitude is the connection to abundance, a practice in acknowledging all we have. It is the avenue through which we receive more. Ironically, when we turn down our consumer-driven "needs", "wants", and "wish lists", we open ourselves to more... more energy, more gifts, and a deeper connection through our heart center. We become an open channel rather than a blocked artery. It is precisely when we find ourselves fixated on lack that we must turn it around. Relief and comfort are right around the corner when we open ourselves to gratitude.

And, with practice, we get good at gratitude... really good. So, let's practice:

Find GRATITUDE as early in the day as possible.

While you're lying in bed or preparing your breakfast, contemplate what you have gratitude for today. Ideally, before you start scrolling through your inbox, text messages, or social media. How you start your day... influences the direction of your day. Pause and reflect... with gratitude for your world and the body you have to experience it.

Eat with GRATITUDE.

Word of the Week

Think of all the people behind the meal you are currently eating... this is one of my favorite practices. Bonus: involve your dining companion(s).

"When eating bamboo sprouts, remember the man who planted them." ~Chinese Proverb

Travel with GRATITUDE.

Air travel, in particular at this time of year, tends to expose us to delays, colds, and full-out grumpiness... turn it around with legitimate appreciation for everyone involved getting you from x to y.

Workout with GRATITUDE.

Best practice. My gratitude journal started in competition prep. It was an essential then because my body was being depleted and asked to do things it normally doesn't have to do (like fasted cardio...). But, even when food is plentiful and an alternative energy source isn't needed, gratitude helps us get more from the workout as we shift our mentality from "have to" to "get to" work out.

Sarah Ingmanson

Pay with GRATITUDE.

The water bill. The electric bill. Every single bill. Especially the ones you don't anticipate. Speeding ticket? ER visit? Yes, bless those, too. Even the exorbitant "this doc saw me for five minutes and charged me what?!" bills.

Exhale GRATITUDE.

In those moments that test your willPower, find gratitude in a great exhale.

Get lost in GRATITUDE.

Backbend. There are so many ways gratitude can permeate your life. Get creative and yes, get lost in it!

Word of the Week

Write (or type) GRATITUDE down.

Keep it in a special notebook or day planner, create a list in your iPad, jot it down on the napkin at Starbucks… just find some space and declare your gratitude.

Minimum 10 "I feel so blessed for…" statements. Every day, don't stop until you hit 10. And feel free to keep going if you're on an inspirational roll. Try to be unique each day. This is not a superstitious act so you don't have to include everything or all the big stuff. Go on a tangent with whatever is happening in your life… in the world… or just on your breakfast plate. Cold outside? Love a fire in the fireplace or warm fuzzy socks? Thanksgiving this week? Grateful for a day off? Grateful for pants with an elastic waistband? Yes, me, too!

Sarah Ingmanson

Meditate with GRATITUDE.

When you're having a hard time settling into meditation, go to gratitude. Allow gratitude to ground you and soothe away the competing thoughts and to-do list.

willPower

Choose to be strong.... willPower

>willPower is being strong when you have to be, but it is also being strong when you *choose* to be.

Life makes you lift heavy things. When you think about the word, willPower, think of it as a practice, a lifestyle, a necessity on occasion, but, most brilliantly, as a choice. Our personal choice.

There are times in our life when we have no choice but to be strong. The death of a loved one, an accident, an illness, a job layoff... times when we are caught off guard, we almost always surprise ourselves with just how strong we are. But, we have to be... in order to make it through... to survive literally or figuratively. These times become important memories as they remind us of ourselves and our true willPower. But, "when we have to" isn't an everyday occurrence, and moreover, it undermines the opportunity to mobilize our personal power to an effective cause... that is, ourselves and this life.

So, what are you waiting for? Beyond the silly excuses you tell yourself, this situation will not get better until you put on your "big girl" panties and decide this is simply not acceptable. You were not born to be dulled down. To be muted. And, you were certainly not born to be slammed against the wall. You are in a holding pattern, hovering over your life, waiting for your willPower to kick in.

willPower is contagious. willPower is a blessing. But, with free will involved, willPower is a choice. Honor that choice. It's a great one to have.

Eat for willPower.

If you want to build strength, then you must eat... and quality protein fuels our muscles. Bison, shrimp, scallops, salmon, tofu, egg whites, oysters, turkey, chicken. Use whey protein powder as convenience when on-the-go.

Have fun with willPower.

This need not be a drag-yourself-through week. Call yourself out with challenges today. Make that phone call. Sign up for that race. Go to a different grocery store, restaurant, cafe... country? Yes, just try something new and watch how your body responds. Be brave and see how each attempt—successful or not—simply builds your confidence.

Move for willPower.

Take a class at the gym. Go for a brisk walk. Figure skate. Ski. Take a ballroom dancing lesson. So many options. Which one(s) appeal to your willPower today?

Plank for willPower... every day.

If you are new to the plank, start with 30 seconds and see if you can work yourself up to two minutes by the end of the year. Experienced plankers, start with two minutes and aim for 5-10 minutes by the end of the year. Daily practice encourages us through progress. We need to recognize just how strong we are...

Ignite your willPower.

What fires you up (in a positive sense)? In my career as an investment banker, I would often receive calls from current students attending my alma mater motivated by the salary, the parents' validation, etc. of working on Wall Street. When I encountered the rare student who shared my passion, it reignited mine. It's fun to run into someone who speaks your language and shares your passion. Seek those people out. Build your tribe and serve as a welcome beacon to the next generation as well.

Encourage someone else's willPower.

We overlook at how influential we are in each other's life experience. When you notice something positive in another, do not hesitate to mention it. What seems so obvious to us is more often than not unrealized in that individual. We tend to undervalue ourselves. So, when we are recognized by another, it strengthens us. Be that person to strengthen another.

Speak with willPower.

Eliminate the "I'll try", "I hope", and "I wish"'s from your vocabulary. Replace these with "I will", "I intend", "I am", and, my personal favorite from a certain amazing instructor (Stacey Lei Krauss), "Self...I got this. I GOT this!" Your body hears everything you say. Change your inner dialog and watch your world transform.

Breathe with willPower.

Shallow breathing is an epidemic failure. This is why meditation is transcending from yoga studios to executive suites. We don't even notice that we are breathing in a shallow manner... until we breathe deeply. Start or keep up that meditation practice and exhale when life calls for it. (Heavy weight or not.)

Be inspired with willPower.

Inspiring stories are all around us. Open your eyes to them and let them lift you. We are all connected. This power lifts us up because we start to realize what is possible for each and every one of us.

Sarah Ingmanson

Journal for willPower.

As you go through your day, write down coincidences, random things that catch your attention, desires you hold in your heart. Actively work to unlock your willPower... and say aloha to your freedom.

GRACE

I humbly receive... GRACE

In Japan, いただきます (*itadakimasu*) is said before every meal. "I humbly receive." This epitomizes grace: intentionally vague and in honorific form.

There is an unfolding in everything we receive. This can be quite difficult to see when our stomachs are in knots and we have no clue what tomorrow will bring. Yet, it is essential to lose our judgement over what-is and instead, receive the moment with grace. For what appears from our limited view to be a storm cloud is actually the beginning of a rainbow. The most beautiful things come out of destruction. So, welcome the destruction and unveil the beauty. The key to surviving the destruction then is to operate with grace.

Blessings are a birthright. There is no deserving or worthiness inherent. It's a manner of receiving that draws them to you.

What we receive is sometimes beyond our earthly understanding, which is why it's important to express our grace honorifically. We acknowledge that even tragedy has universal perfection. Hard to see and feel when we are wrapped up in the emotion of it, but eventually, we may see it... if we open our eyes. Yes, it's easy to misunderstand the divine order, so we must practice grace:

Eat with GRACE.

What does that mean for you? Do you take a moment to honor the meal before eating. Do you eat more delicately, deliberately, or slowly?

Move with GRACE.

Lighten your step, soften your eye gaze. Experience tranquility in your daily movement. Notice how it feels and changes the rest of your day.

Word of the Week

Work out with GRACE.

Ahh my favorite. We might think in terms of getting the workout in and going through the motions. But when we workout with grace... real change occurs because we start from within. We connect the physical to the spiritual, which energizes and lifts. Lose the pre-workout chemical supplement. Find inner energy instead.

Share space with GRACE.

Whether it's on the subway or in line at your grocery store, lose the aggravation of inconvenience, and recognize the freedom in it.

Respond with GRACE.

Sarah Ingmanson

Know the difference between reacting and responding. Take however many moments you need. Lose the self-imposed pressure to be immediate. What is technologically feasible is not necessarily in your best interest.

Speak with GRACE.

Pause and be thoughtful. Not everything needs to be said right now. In fact, most things do not... especially on Facebook!

"If animals could speak, the dog would be a blundering outspoken fellow; but the cat would have the rare grace of never saying a word too much." ~ Mark Twain

Listen with GRACE.

How are you connecting in your conversations? How can you connect one level deeper? Notice your eye contact, your body language, and your intention. With an intention to serve, does your listening change?

Word of the Week

Visualize GRACE.

Close your eyes and see it. Linger there as long as you like. What images comes to your mind? How does it make you feel?

Write with GRACE.

Preserve the art of writing with a handwritten Christmas card, a simple thank-you note, or even just a post-it left out for yourself or loved one.

Above all, invite GRACE in whenever and wherever...

"All the natural movements of the soul are controlled by laws analogous to those of physical gravity. Grace is the only exception. Grace fills empty spaces, but it can only enter where there is a void to receive it, and it is grace itself which makes this void. The imagination is continually at work filling up all the fissures through which grace might pass." ~Simone Weil

PREPARE

Before the body, mind the "mind"... PREPARE

The excitement of something new can wane. When passion stalls, results stall, and then we lose in every way imaginable. So, before you start prepping meals, lists, or any activity, prep your mind.

Don't start until you're ready.

It's a feeling inside. No sense of beginning until you have it. When you're not ready, motivation lacks and the body resists. Meditate. Ground yourself. Identify what moves you and pay attention to the inspiration all around you. Your body will follow your mind.

Word of the Week

Love thyself.

Don't pop pills, starve yourself, or beat yourself up at the gym. Eat high quality foods, lift heavy things, and engage your mind and body with thoughtful intention and dedication... because you love yourself... and your xx-year old body. By treating yourself with kindness and respect, you cultivate longevity... quality longevity.

Steer clear of the have-nots or hardships.

When we harp on how difficult it is (whatever "it" is), results slow to a halt, pounds stick, eyes appear dull, fatigue accumulates, and we attract more struggle. Our internal reward system takes note as well.

If we intrinsically like what we are doing, we feel less need to reward ourselves... because we are already in a happy place. If we perceive total drudgery, we bust out the booze, the pizza, the credit card... because our minds are signaling to our bodies to self-medicate.

Love exactly where you are (vs. where you *were* or where you *want* to be).

Find the novelties and niceties of this day... no matter how trivial. ("I am grateful for this cup of coffee" has made my list MANY times!) Why is life good right where you are? Jot it down if you can. Otherwise, make a mental list as you drive to work... or as you rock your baby to sleep. Gratitude accelerates everything.

Find solutions, not excuses.

We all have busy schedules and different constraints. Instead of saying, "I can't because...", figure out how you can. If you allow your desire to grow sufficiently strong, you will find a way.

Connect this mini-journey to your life journey.

Connection makes the new task integral to or symbolic in your life. It can connect forward or back.

SAVOR

SAVOR... and Save Yourself

Around the holidays, many of us take one of two approaches: deprivation or indulgence. Deprivation results in yearning, perhaps envy, and often a higher-than-thou attitude toward the indulgers. The indulgent ones may experience shame or guilt, and annoyance with the deprivers.

Neither one feels good and yet, the holidays are supposed to feel good. So, as an alternative to deprivation or overindulgence, I invite you to savor. Savor is closer to indulge, but does not rhyme with bulge (bonus) and does not necessarily involve egg nog, chocolate santas, or apple pie... but it *can* (bonus).

Notice you can also savor a sunset or a good heart-to-heart with your favorite uncle, but you would never indulge in these things. When we savor, we appreciate. We don't count calories or call it a cheat meal. We conjure up happiness in that bite, sip, aroma... moment. We recognize the impermanance of life and savor another holiday with our aging parents, grandparents... or a new loved one perhaps. We savor our children at the age they are right now... because it will never be again. And we savor ourselves for what we have created, destructed, and fulfilled this year. We savor and we grow in reverence and in understanding of what is truly important... not the thing, but the act of savoring.

To strengthen willPower, we must practice... and this week's is a fun practice. So jump in and SAVOR it all.

Get nostalgic.

Think back on the holidays when you were a kid. What traditions can you recreate this week?

Get outside. Brisk cold air. Snow. Or, if you're in Vegas, some well-needed Vitamin D.

Pamper yourself.

Massage, foot reflexology, pedicure... good old-fashioned hand-holding. The sense of touch is one to be savored.

Take a nap. Honor the seasonal urge to hibernate.

If you're taking time off from work, actually take it. Don't remote in. Don't check your email any more than you need to. This is your time to nourish and rejuvenate. Savor it!

Take advantage of time off.

Hit the gym in the morning... try a new class. Or maybe, you're away, and you get a different type of workout... like a ski slope or a jog around a new neighborhood. Take it... your body craves movement, and you can savor the contrast between work week and holiday week.

Connect without condition or attachment.

Simply because. That's how we connect… through our heart center. In Heart-2-Heart plank—set the intention with your whole being to savor your life today.

Use music to "put you in the mood".

My iheartradio app plays Christmas music continuously without interruption. What music puts you in the mood you wish to be in?

Be vigilant about your attention.

Notice when your thoughts are fixated on work, future or past events, and gently guide them back to what you are (actually) doing.

Sarah Ingmanson

Journal about how you're feeling. Tell somebody. Take a pic.

Just be sure to capture it somehow. Life becomes more precious when you acknowledge and honor your feelings.

Sarah is a fitness studio owner, Japan specialist, and master presenter of The willPower Method®. She is a former investment banker, nationally-ranked fitness competitor, Fulbright Scholar, and professional figure skater. Sarah received her MBA from Wharton and MA in International Affairs from the Lauder Institute. She won the 2004 Thesis Prize for her master's dissertation, "Corporate Pension Reform in Japan: Big Bang or Big Bust?" Sarah graduated Summa Cum Laude from Tufts University in Quantitative Economics and International Relations.

In 2006, Sarah's frequent flier miles seemed to be accumulating at a rate similar to her ER visits. From Las Vegas to Tokyo to NY, she couldn't seem to manage a business trip without frequenting the Emergency Room even though, by all outward appearances, she was a fit, healthy, happy, and successful woman in her early thirties.

"Outward appearances can be deceiving. When your soul knows differently, your body eventually decides it will no longer put up with the abuse this disconnect is creating. When we are misaligned with our purpose, a part of ourselves dies. Enter willPower here. (Yes, that's willPower with a capital "P".)" ~Sarah Ingmanson

As a framework for unlocking your willPower and developed from The willPower Method®'s "Word of the Week", this book encourages you to think about the parts of yourself... your energy centers... your archetypes. By applying this framework to the Word of the Week, you will bring more deliberate focus to your willPower... and to perhaps the disconnect that is keeping you from true mind-body connection and soul alignment with your life purpose.

Sarah resides in Las Vegas with her husband, Michael, and one-year old daughter, Desiree. Having just opened doors to Star's Locker, a unique dual-studio concept in Las Vegas where fitness becomes a source of empowerment, not punishment, Sarah is bringing willPower to real life... her real life! www.starslocker.com Dream Big. Desire More.